The Cloud of Unknowing

Spiritual commentary by

Dennis J. Billy, CSsR

Liguori
LIGUORI, MISSOURI

Imprimi Potest:
Harry Grile, CSsR, Provincial
Denver Province, The Redemptorists

Published by Liguori Publications
Liguori, Missouri 63057

To order, visit Liguori.org or call 800-325-9521.

Cataloging-in-Publication Data is on file with the Library of Congress.

p ISBN 978-0-7648-2288-9
e ISBN 978-0-7648-6899-3

Liguori Publications, a nonprofit corporation, is an apostolate of The Redemptorists. To learn more about The Redemptorists, visit Redemptorists.com.

Printed in the United States of America
18 17 16 15 14 / 5 4 3 2 1
First Edition

*For all who yearn
to see the face of God*

AND if you are to come to this cloud and dwell and work in it, as I suggest, then just as this cloud of unknowing is above you, that is, between you and your God, so must you also put a cloud of forgetting beneath you and all creation.

From *The Cloud of Unknowing*

Contents

Introduction

The Cloud of Unknowing is an anonymous treatise of Christian mysticism written in Middle English in the latter half of the fourteenth century. Internal evidence suggests the author had a monastic (and possibly priestly) background, with a deep experience of the solitary life. The treatise is addressed to an aspiring contemplative who has already made some progress in the spiritual life and was probably a monk himself interested in learning to contemplate by what he calls "the way of unknowing."

The treatise is significant not only as a classic of Western Christian spirituality in its own right but also as the inspiration for the Centering Prayer movement founded by the Trappist monks Thomas Keating, William Meninger, and M. Basil Pennington. According to Keating, centering prayer is simply "an attempt to present the teaching of earlier times in an updated format and to put a certain order and regularity into it." It is "the experience of interior silence or 'resting in God.'" It focuses on a sacred word and follows this basic principle: "Resist no thought, hang on to no thought, react emotionally to no thought. Whatever image, feeling, reflection or experience attracts your attention, return to the sacred word." [1]

Mystical Roots

The Cloud's approach to Christian prayer has its roots in *Mystical Theology*, a work written in Greek in the late fifth or early sixth century by an anonymous Christian (possibly Syrian) monk under the pseudonym of Dionysius the Areopagite, the person converted by the Apostle Paul at the Areopagus of Athens in the Acts of the Apostles, chapter 17. [2] The key insight of this work is the inaccessibility of God through human thought and the importance of approaching him by way of negation.

The author of *The Cloud* presents his work as a faithful summary of the Areopagite's mystical teaching: "…Whoever reads Dionysius' works will find that he clearly endorses all I have said or shall say from the beginning of this treatise to the end."[3] Although he did not have access to the full Dionysian corpus and came to know much of it only through secondary sources, his deep reliance on this ancient form of Christian mysticism is clear and indisputable.

The God of The Cloud

The author of *The Cloud* prefaces his treatise with a prayer and opens his prologue with the Sign of the Cross, making it clear from the outset that he embraces the classical Christian doctrine of the Trinity. He also affirms his belief in the divinity of Christ, accepts the revealed truths of Christian revelation as his starting point, and views mystical experience as a gift that God bestows on certain individuals for the good of the whole.

The treatise must be read against this backdrop of Christian truths about the nature of God; humanity's creation in God's image and likeness; the consequences of its fall from grace; its redemption made possible by the passion, death, and resurrection of Christ; and its mediation to us through the Church and its sacraments. These beliefs lie at the heart of the work and cannot be stripped from it like some external veneer that reveals some deeper truth or hidden beauty. To do so (or even attempt it) would lead to a serious misreading of the author's intent and purpose.

Rather than denying these truths, the author of *The Cloud* embraces them and shows the reader how to derive from them a deeply contemplative outlook on life, the ultimate goal of which is the face-to-face experience of the divine. Although he recognizes that not everyone is called to a life of pure contemplation, he offers clear instructions for those who are. He begins by identifying four degrees of the Christian life: the ordinary, the special, the solitary, and the perfect. While the first three begin and end in this life, the fourth begins in the present and ends in the world to come. For our anonymous author, the life of pure contemplation offers a foretaste of the beatific vision and thus represents the highest form possible of earthly existence. All other forms of Christian life point toward it and ultimately surpass it in the vision of God.

The Way of Unknowing

Two of the central themes of *The Cloud* are the divine transcendence and its inaccessibility through human thought. Knowledge of God comes not through the kataphatic (or positive) way of ideas, but through the apophatic (or negative) way of self-emptying—hence the phrase "the way of unknowing."

Those of us who wish to experience the divine essence must abandon the way of the intellect and approach God through the way of the heart. We do so by casting every thought that comes to us into "the cloud of forgetting" and by beating with persistent, heartfelt love on "the cloud of unknowing" that separates us from God. Reason has no hope of penetrating the impermeable cloud of darkness separating us from our Creator. Love for God alone has the only hope of piercing it, and it happens (if at all) only because—moved by our heartfelt expressions of love—God himself reaches out to us from the other side.

The author's constant refrain in *The Cloud* is to cast all thought into "the cloud of forgetting" and to beat constantly against "the cloud of unknowing" with the heartfelt longing within our hearts. We do so by focusing our minds on a single word, such as "God" or "love," and using it as a shield against all distracting thoughts and images. When we find ourselves distracted (as often happens with beginners and even the most accomplished contemplatives), we are directed to simply let go of the distraction and return to the word we have chosen, repeating it again and again as a means of knocking against the door of God's heart. This constant beating against "the cloud of unknowing" reveals the depths of our love for God. The more we love God, the more will we desire to contemplate his face, and the more we will beat against the dark, impermeable cloud that separates us from him.

The Spirituality of Unknowing

The spirituality of *The Cloud* is not for everyone. It's only for those who have already made progress in the life of prayer and feel called to live the Gospel on an even deeper level of awareness. The work it describes cannot be achieved through intellectual study or the imaginative faculty and should only be practiced by those called to it. It requires deep humility and total commitment of one's life.

Those desiring pure contemplation must pursue the three-fold way of purgation, illumination, and union. These stages in the spiritual life have three emphases: the purgative focuses on the cleansing of sin; the illuminative, on growth in the virtues; and the unitive, on mystical union with God. The author of *The Cloud* makes it clear that the person who undertakes the work of pure contemplation must have a clear conscience, seek forgiveness through the prescribed means, and make a point of judging no one. Dedication to this work of love requires the gift of God's grace and will eventually calm our sinful inclinations and instill a life of virtue.

In developing his spirituality, the author often refers to Martha and Mary, two New Testament figures who in the Church's tradition, symbolize the active and contemplative lives, respectively. Like Mary, who sat at her Lord's feet instead of helping her sister prepare the meal (see Luke 10:38–42), those called to a life of pure contemplation are often misunderstood and, at times, even criticized by those in the active life. The author explains the roots of this misunderstanding and encourages contemplatives to be understanding and compassionate in their dealings with those who neither understand nor appreciate their calling.

Those who receive the grace of pure contemplation, moreover, must not presume that others will have his or her exact experience. Finite minds cannot contain the infinite nature of the divine, and words used to express mystical experience often conceal as much (if not more) as they reveal. The way of pure contemplation lies in casting all thought into "the cloud of forgetting" and in pounding incessantly on "the cloud of unknowing." When sinful thoughts and impulses come, the author advises those just beginning the work of pure contemplation to look beyond them as though searching for something else or to tremble in their presence and surrender humbly to the power and mercy of God. Beginning contemplatives, moreover, should devote themselves to the reading, reflection, and prayer of *lectio divina* and use short, fervent prayers as a way of piecing the cloud and touching heaven. This method calms reason and will, the principal powers of the soul, and quiets the secondary powers of imagination and sensuality, which have become unruly as a result of original sin.

The author also shows how the grace of contemplation was prefigured in the Ark of the Covenant through Moses, the prophet who was instructed about how it should be made; Bezalel, the craftsman who constructed it; and Aaron, the high priest who could enter its presence at will (see Exodus 38:22; 40:13). He places himself in the office of Bezalel, that is, as someone who constructs something for the benefit of others. He then lists a number of concrete signs by which a person may test whether he or she is called to the work of pure contemplation. Besides cleansing one's conscience, one must have the approval of one's spiritual director, a continuous, pressing desire to practice it, a deep sense that nothing else one does is as important, an even deeper desire to practice it when the experience returns after a long absence, and more joy in finding it than in losing it. The author ends his treatise with the (modernized) words of St. Augustine: "The life of a good Christian consists of nothing else but holy desire." [4]

How to Read The Cloud of Unknowing

The author provides some very specific instructions about who should read his treatise and how it should be read. He states in his *Prologue* that he wrote his book not for the merely curious (whether learned or unlearned) or those who "bicker, flatter, blame, gossip, tattle, tell tales, or steal." [5] Even if they are accomplished in the active life, such people will gain little from what he has written. He wants his work to find its way only into the hands of those who are determined to be perfect followers of Christ and who are preparing for contemplation by cultivating the life of the virtues. Those in the active life may benefit from it but only if they are genuinely interested in deepening their experience of God through the exercise of contemplation.

Later in the prologue, and again in chapter seventy-four, he states that his work should be read several times over and in its entirety, since some things are not fully explained until much later. In keeping with the contemplative nature of the work, moreover, he suggests that his work be read in the fashion of *lectio divina* and only by those with a true affinity for a life of pure contemplation. This slow, meditative reading goes through the text not merely for content but for the deep spiritual wisdom beneath its surface. For this to happen, we must chew the text and digest it by reading it, reflecting upon it, praying over it, and resting in it.

The present volume adapts Evelyn Underhill's 1922 edition of *The Cloud*[6] to our modern English idiom. This adaptation—which includes the author's brief chapter summary at the start of each chapter and features the first word or so of the text in all capital letters—seeks to remain faithful to the text while making it more accessible to today's readers. Using italicized type, I have added appropriate background and reflection questions to each of the treatise's seventy-five chapters to help readers engage the text in a more dynamic and personal way. The anonymous author's prayer and prologue also feature introductions and questions. Readers should go through this work slowly and use the introductions and reflection questions as a way of entering more deeply into the text and allowing it to open their minds and hearts to the way of unknowing. They are also encouraged to read the text not for in-formation but as a topic for meditative reflection. They will benefit from it more by spending twenty minutes in quiet reflection each day on a single chapter than by going through the entire work quickly in a single sitting. This quiet, meditative reading of the text will help foster in them a contemplative attitude toward life and help them follow the way of unknowing in their daily lives.

Conclusion

Our purpose in reading a book such as *The Cloud* is not to lose ourselves in a nostalgic recreation of a distant (and ultimately irretrievable) medieval religious landscape, but to explore that past in order to find helpful insights for dealing with our present spiritual struggles. Such insights encourage us to enter into a dialogue with the text still further and to become aware of our own feelings and judgments about the meaning of our spiritual journey. In doing so, we will doubtless find ourselves, at times, both questioning its teaching and being questioned by it. This dynamic relationship between the text and its reader touches the very heart of spiritual reading and is extremely important when dealing with this classic of Christian spirituality.

Some twenty years ago, William A. Meninger, OCSO, one of the founders of the Centering Prayer movement, paid this eloquent tribute to the treatise:

> For more than twenty-five years I have been giving retreats and workshops on contemplative prayer as taught by a fourteenth-century book called *The Cloud of Unknowing* by an unknown English author. Inspired myself by the loving union with God that *The Cloud* teaches, I have been blessed with the privilege of teaching it to thousands of others. I have read *The Cloud* more than a hundred times, and each time I find it a new book, a new inspiration, a source of new ideas about the "work of love" (the descriptive phrase *The Cloud* uses to describe contemplative prayer!) or "the loving search," as I call it herein. [7]

May this new edition and commentary on *The Cloud* be for you at all times "a new book, a new inspiration, a source of new ideas about the 'work of love.'" May it guide you in the way of the unknowing, fill your heart with love, and bring you to the threshold of a face-to-face encounter with the divine.

DENNIS J. BILLY, CSsR

Here begins a book of contemplation

called *The Cloud of Unknowing*,

in which a soul is made one with God.

Background

The author begins his work with a prayer that was well-known in the Carthusian Charter Houses of his day, leading some scholars to speculate from this and other internal evidence that the author himself was a member of that renowned order of hermits. He changes the wording of the prayer somewhat, but not in a way that would draw undue attention.[8] The prayer opens with an address to God, telling him that nothing can be hidden from him, that he can probe all human hearts, and that he can see their deepest intentions and desires. The author then petitions God for two things: a purification of his heart and the gift of grace, two essential themes in the work that is to follow. Purification (or detachment from earthly things) is a basic prerequisite for the grace of union with God—the ability to love him to the fullest and praise him as he deserves.

TEXT

O GOD,
from whom nothing is hidden,
and who peers into all hearts
and speaks to them,
I ask you to cleanse my heart's intentions
with the gift of your grace
so I may love you perfectly
and praise you worthily.
Amen.

Entering the Cloud

- *Do you believe that God sees into your heart and knows your deepest intentions and desires? How does this make you feel? Uneasy? Hesitant? Afraid? Peaceful? Does this possibility that God sees deep within you increase or decrease your love for God?*

- *Do you believe that God can purify your heart? What does your heart need to cleansed of?*

- *Is there anything in your life that you are trying to hide from God? If so, what is it? How can you unburden yourself of this heavy load? Confession? Prayer? Doing good to others?*

- *Why confess to God something that he already knows? Does it have something to do with entering into deeper intimacy through an authentic sharing of self?*

- *Do you believe that God can pour grace into your heart to help you love and praise him more deeply? Is there anything holding you back or keeping you from asking for this grace?*

Prologue

Background

The author introduces his seventy-five chapters on the cloud of unknowing with a prologue. He opens this with a brief prayer, where he clearly identifies the God of whom he speaks as the Holy Trinity. He then turns his attention to those who may come into possession of his work. He states that the contents of the work are very deep and addressed to a particular group of people, those desiring to lead a life of pure contemplation. In his mind (and according to monastic tradition), this state represents the highest form of Christian living, since it makes one a perfect follower of Christ. He begs those who do not fall into this category not to read it, either alone or in a group, and certainly not to copy it. He is concerned only with the life of pure contemplation. At the same time, he recognizes that some in the active life have been preparing to enter this stage for some time through the practice of the virtues and other exercises. He welcomes these people as eager readers. He points out, however, that many in the active life are not called to this higher calling (at least, not in this life). His work, he says, is not for them. He then tempers his request somewhat by asking those who insist on reading his book to do so to the very end, since some things in it are not fully explained until later on. People not reading it all the way through run the risk of misunderstanding and possibly even falling into error. On another note, he clearly states that he has no time for those who "bicker, flatter, blame (either themselves or others), gossip, tattle, tell tales, or steal." Nor does he want any interference from cynics or from calculating clergy or lay people who may be skilled in the ways of the active life but have no desire or yearning to delve into the mysterious cloud of unknowing. He wants his work to be read only by those who desire perfection and who see the contemplative life as the highest expression of the life of discipleship. After this

19

heartfelt exhortation, the author concludes his prologue with a brief description of the structure of the work: seventy-five chapters, the last of which indicates some key signs that a person is being called to a life of pure contemplation. He follows with a table of chapters.

TEXT

IN the name of the Father and of the Son and of the Holy Spirit.

Whoever is in possession of this book—as an owner, a curator, a messenger, or a borrower—I charge and implore you with all the power and strength that the bond of love allows that you neither read it, nor copy it, nor recite it, nor allow it to be read, copied, or recited by anyone who is not in both will and intention a true follower of Christ. This person should be accomplished not only in the active life but also in the contemplative, which is possible during this earthly sojourn through grace. Do your best to see that this person has persevered in the rigorous demands of the active life, for otherwise it will be of little help. Also, I charge and implore you, with love's authority, that if anyone should read it, copy it, recite it, or else hear it read or recited, that you ask him as I ask you, to take the time to read it, recite it, copy it, or hear it in its entirety. For something may be unclear at the beginning or middle and not fully explained until later or at the book's end. Therefore, someone, on seeing only a part of the truth, may be easily led into error. Therefore, to avoid such errors both in yourself and in others, I ask you—out of love—to do as I say.

I do not care if those who bicker, flatter, blame (either themselves or others), gossip, tattle, tell tales, or steal ever see this book. I did not write it for them, and I would prefer if they did not meddle with it. In addition, I would include any of the merely curious, be they learned or unlearned. Although they may be good in the active life, this book will accord them nothing. At the same time, there are those who follow the active life yet are graciously disposed to contemplation through the inward stirring and hidden designs of God's Spirit. Even though, unlike experienced contemplatives, they are not continually disposed to contemplation but receive only occasional insights into this highest form of prayer, upon seeing this work they should by God's grace be greatly comforted by it.

This book is divided into seventy-five chapters. Of these, the last teaches certain signs by which a person may tell whether he or she is called by God to this work of contemplation.

Spiritual friend in God, I beg and beseech you to be attentive to the direction and manner of your vocation. Give heartfelt thanks to God so that, with the help of His grace, you may persevere in the state, stage, and way of life you have chosen, against all the devious assaults of your physical and spiritual enemies, and so win the crown that lasts forever. Amen.

Entering the Cloud

- *Do you believe in the triune God? Do you sense that the author, at the very outset, is warning his readers that he is seeking to probe the mystery of the Godhead and enter into the deepest dimension of its being?*

- *Do you understand why he wants only certain people to read his work: those wishing to live a life of contemplation and to become perfect followers of Christ? Do you think you fall into this category? Are you already living a life of pure contemplation? Are you living an active life, yet yearning for something more: a deeper union with God?*

- *Is this work for you? Do you think you should read it?*

- *Are you willing to read it to the very end? Are you willing to allow it to speak not just to your mind but also your heart?*

- *Do you sense how, from the very beginning, the author seeks to root his work firmly in the Christian tradition?*

A Table of the Chapters

Chapter One

*The four degrees of Christian living and how the call came
to the one for whom this book was written.*

Background

The author writes chapter one as an introduction, where he addresses his work to a "spiritual friend," someone who was most likely a beginner in the solitary life yet with a deep desire to make progress in the way of contemplation. The use of "spiritual friend" could also be a literary device, one not unknown in the monastic tradition of the day, whose purpose was to establish an immediate spiritual bond between the author and his readers. However it is taken, the author reviews for his friend (real or otherwise) the four degrees of Christian life: the ordinary (for the laity), the special (for religious and clerics), the solitary (for hermits), and the perfect (for pure contemplatives). [9] He tells his friend that the first three begin and end in this life, while the fourth can start in this life but reaches its fulfillment only in the next. He tells his friend that God has called him along all of these different stages, first as a lay person, then as a religious or cleric, then as a hermit, and now as a pure contemplative. This reference to the hermitical life as a third and higher form of life suggests that the work was intended for a Carthusian. With the exception of this group of solitaries, the monastic orders of the day generally did not leave the communal life of the order for a hermitage. [10] The author tells his friend that, after having been called to live the life of a hermit, the allure of God's grace has stirred in him a longing for something still deeper, a yearning for God that leads to union with and a direct, experiential knowledge of him. He then encourages his friend to begin the journey to perfection by lifting the foot of his love and beginning his journey toward the final state of living, the way of pure contemplation.

Text

SPIRITUAL friend in God, I find in my busy mind four degrees and forms of Christian life: the common, the special, the solitary, and the perfect. Three of them begin and end in this life, while the fourth begins here by grace but continues without end in the bliss of heaven. And just as you see them set down in order one after another—first the common, then the special, then the solitary, and then the perfect—so I think our Lord has called you out of His great mercy in the same order and led you to Himself by the desire of your heart. Know that, when you were in the common state of Christian living in the company of your friends in the world, the everlasting love of His divinity through which He made you when you were nothing and bought you with the price of His precious blood when you were lost in Adam, would not allow you to be so distant from Him in state and kind. And so He kindled your desire with the fullness of grace and fastened to it a leash of longing and led you by it into a more special way of living: to be a servant among His special servants, where you might learn to live more intensely and spiritually in His service than you did before, or might have done, when in the common state of life.

Furthermore, such was the love of His heart for you that He was not content to leave you like this. For what did He do? Do you not see how graciously He has secretly pulled you to the third degree and manner of life? In this state, the solitary form and manner of living, you learned to take your first step of love toward the final state and kind of living, the perfect.

Entering the Cloud

- *Do you consider yourself a beginner in the spiritual life? A beginner in the active life? A beginner in the contemplative life?*

- *Where would you place yourself in the various degrees of Christian life that the author sets out?*

- *Does the author associate the degrees of the spiritual life too closely with the various states of life within the Church? That is to say, are members of the first three stages entirely excluded from the possibility of reaching the state of pure contemplation or must they leave these states behind? What does your experience tell you?*

- *Have you ever felt the allure of God's grace to enter into a deeper relationship with him?*

- *Have you ever felt the duties and responsibilities of your present state in life holding you back or preventing you from achieving a deeper relationship with God?*

- *Is it possible to receive the call to pure contemplation apart from the call to the solitary life?*

- *What role does solitude play in your own spiritual life? Is it possible for you to find a quiet place in your heart, a place of solitude, where you can allow God's grace to quietly work?*

- *What challenges or obstacles does your present state in life set before you in your quest for God? Do you bring these to God in prayer and seek his guidance?*

Chapter Two

An urgent call to humility and the work of contemplation.

Background

In this chapter, the author asks us to face the truth about ourselves. We are nothing but weak, fragile creatures, easily prone to sin. Because our hearts are impoverished and our souls numbed by sleep and laziness, we are unable to respond to the alluring power of God's love. We are unable, moreover, to listen to that still small voice within us calling us to a deeper union with God. The author calls us to humility. He tells us not to think ourselves special because of our state in life but to be conscious of our littleness and smallness before God and others. He exhorts us to be meek and loving as Jesus himself, who humbled himself in order to become man. Jesus did so to call disciples to follow his way of pure contemplation, a way that would lead them to the deepest intimacy with God. The author then encourages us to press on and not to worry about what we are leaving behind, for what lies ahead is many times more beautiful and lasting. It is now time for us to allow our desire for God to lead us. This desire comes from God and speaks to the heart. The author asks us to cooperate with this divine grace by embracing it with all our hearts. He also reminds us that God is a jealous lover and allows no other partners. God alone must be the one and only desire of our hearts. The true disciple, therefore, must be purged of all earthly attachments. This can be done by shutting the windows of our souls to the snares of the enemy. All God asks of us is to purge our hearts in this way and to seek him in humble prayer. God is waiting for us at this very moment. All that remains for us is to decide what to do. Will we set out on the way of pure contemplation or settle for less?

TEXT

LOOK up and see what you are. Who are you and what have you merited to be called by our Lord? What weary, impoverished heart, sleeping in sloth, are you who has not awakened to this love and to the voice of this calling! Beware of your enemy and never consider yourself holier or better because of the worthiness of this call and your solitary form of living. You will be poor and accursed unless you do what is good by grace and counsel to live according to your conscience. And to that extent you should be more humble and loving to your spiritual spouse, who is the Almighty God, King of Kings and Lord of Lords, who humbled Himself so low in order to come to you. For among all the sheep of His flock, He graciously chose you to be one of His special ones and set you in a place of pasture, where you might be fed with the sweetness of His love, longing for your heritage, the kingdom of heaven.

Go on then, I beg you earnestly. Look forward, not backward. See what you need and not what you already have, for that is the easiest way of becoming and staying humble. Your whole life must be one of desire, if you are to benefit in this stage of perfection. This desire was placed in your will by the hand of Almighty God with your consent. But let me assure you of one thing: He is a jealous lover and allows no rival. He does not want to work in you unless He is alone with you and has you all to Himself. He does not ask for help. All He wants is you. He is the one who wills, you just need to look at Him and let Him do His work. You must, however, keep the windows and doors of your soul shut against the assailing flies of the enemy. And if you are willing to do this, you need but humbly call upon Him in prayer, and He will soon come to your aid. Press on then, let us see how you carry yourself. He is ready and waits for you. But what will you do and how shall you continue?

Entering the Cloud

- *What is the truth about yourself? Do you think of yourself as a weak and fragile creature easily prone to sin? Or do you think of yourself as someone unique and deserving of special treatment?*

- *Are you perhaps a mixture of the two? If so, which one is more prominent? Which is growing, and which is dying?*

- *What can you learn about humility by Jesus' example of emptying himself to become one of us?*

- *Why is humility, knowing the truth about oneself, so important for the way of discipleship?*

- *Why is humility important for those wishing to respond to the alluring love of God in order to experience him in the deepest throes of contemplation?*

- *Is union with God your deepest desire? Is God your only love? Is there anything getting in the way or holding you back from loving God the way you should?*

- *How can you shut the windows of your soul to the temptations and snares of your enemies? How can you purge your heart for God so that he may fill it with himself?*

- *Are you ready to begin this contemplative journey? Do you really want to? Would you rather stay where you are?*

Chapter Three

How the work of contemplation should be carried out,
and how it is worth more than all other works.

Background

In this chapter, the author gives us a description of the practice that leads toward pure contemplation. This practice involves focusing one's attention entirely on God. To do so, we must first let go of all creature attachments and lose them in what the author calls "the cloud of forgetting." By leaving our earthly lives behind us, we are better able to experience the divine mysteries to which we have been called. Angels and saints, the author tells us, rejoice at its use, since it enables us to stay in close contact with the source of all life and being. Demons and evil spirits, on the other hand, cringe at its use, because it—more than anything else—hinders them from leading us away from God and to a life dedicated to evil and self-centeredness. The author cautions us that we cannot accomplish this task on our own, but we need to cooperate with the movement of God's grace in our hearts. For this reason, he encourages us to ask for this divine grace and to respond to it the moment it comes. He tells us that it will first lead us into a terrible darkness, a cloud of unknowing, which all creatures must experience before they stand before the face of God. In this cloud, it will be impossible for us to see God with our hearts, minds, or affections. We are to rest in this darkness, relying only on our faith as we allow God to probe the deepest recesses of our minds and hearts so that we might be able to enter the cloud more deeply. In this state, we must cry out to God with all our hearts and reach out with our deepest yearnings. God, the source of these longings, will hear them and respond to our deepest wishes.

TEXT

LIFT up your heart to God with a humble movement of love. Seek Him alone and none of His goods. Be resolved to think of nothing but Him so that nothing fills your mind and will but Him alone. Do what you can to forget all the creatures ever made by God and their works so that your thoughts and desires are not directed or extended to any of them either generally or in particular. Let them be and pay no attention to them. This work of the soul pleases God the most. All the angels and saints find joy in this work and hasten to foster it with all their might. All fiends and demons are furious when you do this work, and they try to defeat it in everything they do. Those on earth are greatly helped by this work, although you would not know how. The souls in purgatory are eased of their pain by virtue of this work. You yourself are cleansed and made virtuous by it. And yet when a soul is helped by grace and has a conscious longing, it is the easiest work of all and can be achieved very quickly. Otherwise, it is difficult and beyond your ability.

Do not give up, then, but work at it until you feel this longing. For when you first attempt it, you find nothing but darkness, as if it were a cloud of unknowing. You do not know what it means, except that you feel in your will a naked desire for God. Whatever you do, this darkness and this cloud stand between you and your God. They prevent you from seeing Him clearly by the light of understanding and from feeling the sweetness of His love in your affection.

Therefore, prepare yourself to stay in this darkness as long as is necessary, while crying all along for the one you love. For if you are to feel or see Him in this life, it must always be in this cloud, in this darkness. And if you work hard, as I ask you, I trust in His mercy that you will come to it.

Entering the Cloud

- *Do you think yourself capable of letting go of all creaturely things into the cloud of forgetting so that you can focus all your energies on God?*

- *Are there certain duties and responsibilities in your present state of life that you simply could not leave behind? Do you still feel tied to them? Will they be easy to forget and put aside?*

- *Have you authentically discerned whether God is actually calling you to enter the cloud of unknowing? What would you be giving up? What would you be gaining? What challenges and difficulties will lie ahead for you? Are you really ready to send all creaturely things into the cloud of forgetting—even the people and things you hold most dear?*

- *Are the requirements for entering the cloud of unknowing too much for you? Do they seem a bit overwhelming?*

- *Do you really want God to be the sole master of your heart? Are you able at least to ask him to help you pray for the grace to let go of all creaturely things so that he alone will be your heart's only desire?*

Chapter Four

This work of contemplation is brief, and the experience of it
cannot be acquired by study or imagination.

Background

In this chapter, the author offers a brief description of the kind
of prayer appropriate for entering the cloud of unknowing. He
lays out the necessary practices involved and reminds us that this
form of prayer cannot be achieved by intellectual study or by the
imagination. The union with God that comes through the prayer
of unknowing involves another route, one that is dark and full
of danger and uncertainty. The author does not want anyone to
make any mistakes in the practice of this prayer, so he decides
to say something more about it. First of all, he says that it is not
something that takes an enormous amount of time, as some seem
to think. He likens it to an atom, which the scholars of his day
considered to be the smallest particle of time. These particles are
so small that they seem almost undetectable. If we liken them to
all the movements within our hearts and minds, they would be
infinitesimal, disconnected, and would be almost impossible to
count. The author tells us that God does not abandon us to face
these impulses alone, but he helps us to confront them and deal
with them. He draws us to himself by fitting himself exactly to our
souls. He does so by virtue of his transforming grace and because
he has created us in his own image and likeness. We were made
for God, the author is saying, and God aims to claim his prize.

The author then draws an important distinction between a
person's power to know and the power to love. The author tells us
that God is totally incomprehensible to the first but fully comprehensible to the second by each person. Here, we are talking about
the difference between knowledge about God and knowing him
personally. The author points out that only the way of love sheds

light on the path of the cloud of unknowing. It alone will lead us to God, for this light comes from God himself. The light of the Holy Spirit, who reforms us by grace, helps us to gain control of our impulses and gives us a taste of everlasting sweetness even in this life. Our restoration and transformation to holiness, the author tells us, will take place by the practice of centering our lives entirely on God.

The author tells us, moreover, that we face only one atom or particle of time at a time. By itself, it is not overwhelming, if we are strengthened by God's grace. Still, each particle of time must be taken seriously. We cannot presume on God's help. Heaven, he tells us, can be won or lost in a single moment. Just as the atoms of time are so little, so too are the prayers which meet them and transform them. The author asks us to pay attention to these prayerful inspirations. When correctly understood, they are nothing other than "a sudden urge that comes without warning and quickly springs up to God like a spark from a fire's coals." These short, passionate prayers come from God and are meant to counter the evil impulses of our fallen nature. Such prayers come not by way of intellectual knowledge or the imagination but are expressions of pure love inspired in our hearts by God's grace. The intimate knowledge of God that comes through such prayer begins slowly, hence giving us a sense of being in a cloud of unknowing. If we are faithful to this exercise of prayer, that cloud will dissipate in time and we will experience an intimate union with God far beyond whatever our meager intellects or limited imaginations could even hope to conjure.

TEXT

SO that you may not stumble or err in this matter and wish it were something else, I will tell you a little more about it as I perceive it.

This work does not take a long time to complete, as some think. Indeed, it is the shortest of all that can be conceived! It is not any longer or shorter than an atom, which the philosophers of astronomy will tell you is the smallest part of time. It is so small that it is indivisible and nearly incomprehensible. This is that "time" of which it is written, "You shall be asked how you spent all the time given to you." It is quite reasonable that you should have to account for it. It is neither longer nor shorter than a single movement of your will, the principal power of your soul. For there can be as many movements or desires of your will within a single hour as there are atoms of time. And if you were reformed by grace to the original state of Adam's soul, as it was before the Fall, you would be lord of all those desires. No one would stray. All would reach out to God, the Lord of all desires, who is the summit of all that can be willed. For He meets our soul by limiting His Godhead, and our soul meets Him because we have been created in His image and likeness. He alone is completely and utterly capable of satisfying the will and the desires of our soul. And our soul, when reformed by grace, becomes capable of comprehending Him completely by love. He is incomprehensible to the minds of rational creatures such as angels and men—but not to their love. All rational creatures such as angels and men possess a power of knowing and a power of loving. To the first, God is forever incomprehensible. To the second, however, He is completely comprehensible to each individual. Through its love, a single soul can comprehend Him who, without comparison, is capable of satisfying all the souls in existence. This is the everlasting miracle of love, for God has always worked in this way and forever will. Take account of this, if you can by the grace of God. To experience it personally is endless bliss; its contrary is endless suffering.

Therefore, if any man were so reformed by grace that he heeded every movement of his will, he would never be without some sense of the eternal sweetness, even in this life, nor without its full realization in the bliss of heaven. So do not be astonished if I urge you on in this work of contemplation. As you will hear later, it is precisely what man would be doing today if he had not sinned. Man was made for this, and everything possible was done to help him achieve this end. It is through this that man shall be restored. It is because he does not listen that man falls deeper and deeper into sin and grows further and further from God. Yet it is by constantly listening and attending to this work of contemplation, and nothing else, that a man rises higher and higher from sin and grows closer and closer to God.

So pay attention to time and how you spend it, for there is nothing more precious. In a single moment, small as it is, heaven may be won or lost. Here is a sign that time is precious: God never gives two moments together but always one after another. If He did otherwise, He would need to change the course of creation itself. Time is made for man, not man for time. And God, the Lord of creation, orders time according to human nature so that the natural impulses of the soul occur one at a time. On the day of judgment, man will have no excuse before God when he gives an account of how he spent his time. He cannot say, "You give two times at once, when I have but one impulse at a time."

But now you are laden with sorrow and say, "What am I to do? If what you say is true, how shall I give an account of each moment of time? I am twenty-four years old and entirely disregardful of time! If I changed now, you know very well from what you have already written that there are no moments of time to spare, either in nature or in grace, with which I could make up for my past. I can only work on those moments that are still to come. What is more, I know full well that, because of my deep frailty and lethargy of spirit, I am only able to heed one impulse in a hundred. What a situation I am in! Help me now, for the love of Jesus!"

You are right to say, "for the love of Jesus." For your help is in the love of Jesus. The power of love shares in all things. Love Jesus, therefore, and all that He has is yours. As God, He makes and gives time. As man, He keeps time. As God and man together, He judges how best to spend one's time. Knit yourself to Him by

41

love and faith, and through that knot you will be joined to Him and to everyone united to Him in love. This includes Holy Mary, who was full of grace at every moment in time, all the angels of heaven, who can never lose time, and all the saints in heaven and on earth, who by their love and by Jesus' grace know how to spend their time. There is comfort here. Understand it clearly and profit from it. But let me warn you especially of one thing. I do not see how anyone can claim to be in communion with Jesus and His Mother, His angels and His saints, unless he is doing all he can, with the help of grace, to keep time and to spend it well, so that, along with all the rest, he will be seen as doing his part, small as it is, to strengthen that communion.

So take heed of this marvelous work of grace in your soul. It is always a sudden urge that comes without warning and quickly springs up to God like a spark from a fire's coals. An amazing number of such urges arises in one brief hour in the soul disposed to this work of contemplation. In one such moment, it may suddenly and completely forget the whole created world. Soon afterward, however, because of our corrupted nature, we fall down into thought and the memories of things done and undone. Still afterward, it may rise again within us as suddenly as it did before.

Here is how it works. It is far from any fantasy or false imagination or quaint opinion. These would not come from a devout and humble impulse of love but from a proud, curious, and imaginative mind. If this work of contemplation is truly conceived in purity of spirit, then such a proud, curious mind would always be borne down and stiffly trodden underfoot. For whoever hears or reads about this work of contemplation and thinks that it is an activity of the mind and goes on to work it all out along these lines is greatly deceived. Such a man, whoever he may be, creates an experience that is neither spiritual nor physical and is seriously misled. Unless God, in His great goodness, breaks in with a miracle of mercy and makes him stop and follow the counsel of those who truly understand, he will go mad or suffer some other dreadful form of spiritual harm or demonic deception. Then his life and soul may be easily lost for all eternity. So for the love of God, be wary in this work and do not try to achieve this experience through the intellect or the imagination. I tell you truly, it cannot come through them. So leave them alone.

And do not think that because I call it "darkness" or a "cloud" that it is the kind of cloud you see in the sky or the type of darkness you experience at home on nights when the candle is out. For that kind of darkness or cloud you can picture in your mind's eye in the height of summer, just as in the depth of a winter's night you can picture a clear shining light. This is not what I mean at all. By "darkness" I mean "a lack of knowing," since anything you do not know or have forgotten is "dark" to you, for you cannot see it with your inner eye. For this reason it is called a "cloud," not of the sky, but a cloud of unknowing between you and God.

Entering the Cloud

- *Do you understand the practice of prayer that the author proposes? Have you ever prayed that way before? Are there other types of prayer that you find more suitable?*

- *Do you accept his statement that these brief, fiery darts of passionate prayer are directly inspired by God's grace and are the only way to make your way through the cloud of unknowing?*

- *Do you agree with the author's distinction between a person's power of knowing and power of loving?*

- *Is the author anti-intellectual? What kind of knowledge is he seeking? What kind of knowledge does he have little time for? What kind of knowledge does he hope to gain by entering the cloud of unknowing?*

- *Do you agree with the author's depiction of time as a series of disconnected particles or atoms that must be faced one-by-one and defeated by means of the short but intense ejaculatory prayers God sends us through the cloud of unknowing?*

- *Are you aware of any schools of Christian spirituality that present the way to God differently?*

Chapter Five

*During this work of contemplation, all creatures from the
past, present, or future (and all their works) must be hidden
in the cloud of forgetting.*

Background

In this chapter, the author tells us that, should we enter the cloud
of unknowing, we must make every effort to cast all thoughts
and desires for creaturely things into the cloud of forgetting. He
tells us that we may feel distant from God while in the cloud of
unknowing, for it stands between us and blocks our view of his
divinity. He reminds us, however, that we would be even further
away from him if we had never entered the cloud in the first place
and continued to occupy our thoughts and desires with creaturely
things. Better to forget them and focus all our attention on the
one thing that matters: the strange and elusive God awaiting us
behind the dark, mysterious cloud in which we find ourselves. The
author tells us that in the cloud of forgetting, we should cast not
only all creatures but even their deeds and circumstances. We must
not even occupy ourselves with thoughts of the Blessed Mother,
the angels and saints, or even heaven and its joys. God, and God
alone, should be foremost in our thoughts. Everything else will
hinder our journey through the cloud's dark interior. Only the
surrounding cloud of unknowing should stand between us and
the God we seek.

TEXT

AND if you are to come to this cloud and dwell and work in it, as I suggest, then just as this cloud of unknowing is above you, that is, between you and your God, so must you also put a cloud of forgetting beneath you and all creation. You may think you are very far from God because of this cloud of unknowing between you and God, but surely it would be better to say you would be much further from Him if there were no cloud of forgetting between you and all creation. Whenever I say "all creation," I mean not only the creatures themselves but also all their works and everything related to them. There is no exception, whether they are physical or spiritual beings, or whether we are referring to their condition in life or their actions, or to their goodness or badness. In short, all things must be concealed in this cloud of forgetting.

For although it is sometimes helpful to think of the nature and deeds of individual creatures, in this case it is practically useless. To remember or to think about what a thing is or does has a spiritual effect. Your soul's eye focuses on it, just as a marksman fastens his eye on his target. Consider this: Everything you think about is above and between you and your God. And you are that much more distant from God if anything but God is in your mind.

Indeed, if I may say so without being disrespectful, when engaged in this work you are helped very little (if at all) by thinking of God's kindness or worth, or of our Lady, or of the saints or angels in heaven, or of the joys of heaven. Such meditations that strengthen your sense of purpose will not help you in this work of contemplation. For although it is good to think about the kindness of God and to love Him and praise Him for it, it is much better to consider Him as He is, in His naked being, and to love and praise Him for Himself.

Entering the Cloud

- *Why do created things have the potential to keep us from knowing God? What effect do they have on us that prevents us from giving our full attention to God?*

- *Is the author being too demanding when he asks us to cast all thoughts of creaturely things into the cloud of forgetting? Is it even possible for us to do so?*

- *Does the author present his way as the only way to God? Is he sensitive to other possible paths that will lead to intimacy with God?*

- *Is the path he describes too difficult? Is it meant only for a very select few? Can it be easily misunderstood?*

- *Is the path he lays out meant for you? Are you ready to cast all thoughts of heavenly and earthly things into the cloud of forgetting?*

Chapter Six

A brief review of this work through question and answer.

Background

In this chapter, the author examines us by way of question and answer. How should we think of God? What is he like? He responds by telling us that even he has not the slightest idea. God lies beyond the power of the human intellect. He cannot be experienced, grasped, or pondered like a mere creature. We do not enter the cloud of unknowing in order to attain an intellectual vision of God. We do so in order to love him. We approach God not through the mind but through love. It is through love alone that we can grasp and understand him. Although the author admits that it is sometimes good to think of God's kindness and dignity, and while he recognizes that such actions offer light and are a part of contemplation, he insists that such actions must also be cast into the cloud of forgetting. Love alone can guide us through the dark cloud of unknowing. To move ahead, we must leave all actions of the mind, all acts of the intellect, behind. As we penetrate the cloud, we are to be armed only with the sharpened arrows of our longing love.

TEXT

BUT now you ask me, "How can I think of God in Himself and what He is?" And to this I can only respond, "I do not know."

For your question has brought me into that same darkness and into that same cloud of unknowing that I wish you yourself were in. For although through God's grace we can have full knowledge of all other creatures and their works—and even of the works of God—yet no one can probe God as he is in Himself. I would rather abandon all that I am capable of knowing and choose instead to love the one thing I cannot know through thought. Why? Because God may be loved but not thought. He may be gotten and held by love but not by thought. And therefore, although it may be good sometimes to think of God's kindness and worth in particular, and although it may be a light for us and an aspect of contemplation, nevertheless when you are involved in this work it must be cast down and covered with a cloud of forgetting. You must step over it boldly, yet tearfully, with a devout and pleasing impulse of love and try to pierce that cloud above you. Strike that thick cloud of unknowing with a sharp dart of longing love and refuse to give up.

Entering the Cloud

- *Do you believe that God lies beyond the powers of the human intellect?*

- *Do you believe that our minds have the power to comprehend God fully?*

- *Why does the author say that love, and love alone, has such power? What does the power of love reveal about the nature of God that the intellect fails to perceive?*

- *Do you agree with the author's assessment of the powers of the intellect? Why does he make it secondary to the powers of love?*

- *Is he completely against reason, or is he merely trying to point out its limitations?*

Chapter Seven

How someone should deal with thoughts when involved in this work, especially those that arise from one's own curiosity, cunning, and natural wit.

Background

In this chapter, the author tells us how to treat any thoughts that may enter our mind while we are in the cloud. If they ask us what we seek and what we are looking for, we should say, "God alone, who created us, redeemed us, gives us grace, and calls us to love." He points out that no thoughts, however noble and worthy, can lead us to God. For this reason, we must cast all thoughts into the cloud of forgetting. We must command such thoughts to go away and, if they insist on remaining, we must respond with a simple urge or impulse of love. We can do this by reaching out to God with a simple word that gathers all the love for God we have inside of us. Such a word (like "God" or "love") will help us put aside these distracting thoughts and, with God's help, enable us to penetrate the dark cloud in which we find ourselves.

TEXT

IF any thoughts should arise and interfere continually with you and this darkness, asking what you are seeking and what you want, answer that it is God you want: "Him I desire, Him I seek, nothing but Him."

And if your thoughts ask you, "Who is this God?" answer that it is the God who made you and redeemed you and who has graciously called you to His love. Tell them, moreover, that you know nothing about Him, and then say, "Get down!" and proceed to trample them down with a simple movement of love. Do this even though such thoughts may seem holy and even able to lead you to God. As a result, God may well bring to your mind many beautiful and wonderful thoughts to remind you that He is sweet, loving, gracious, and merciful. He will do this if you but listen to Him. He asks nothing more. He will go on and on conversing with you until He brings you steadily down until you start thinking of His passion.

And there will He let you see the wonderful kindness of God. He only wants you to hear Him. For soon after He will let you see your former way life so that, in seeing and thinking of it, He will help you recall some place you have lived before. And before you know it you will be broken and scattered beyond belief. The cause of this brokenness will be that you heard Him freely and then answered Him, received Him, and finally let Him alone to do His work in you.

And yet the thoughts we are talking about are both good and holy, so holy that no man or woman can hope to achieve contemplation without many such meditations of their own inner poverty, the Lord's passion, the kindness of God, and of His great goodness and worth. Still, someone long practiced in these meditations must leave them behind. He must put them down and cast them into the cloud of forgetting if he is ever to penetrate the cloud of unknowing between him and his God. So when you feel by God's grace that He is calling you to this work, and you decide to respond, lift up your heart to God with a humble movement of love. And really decide for God Himself, who created you, redeemed you, and has graciously called you to this state of life. And receive no other thought but God. It all depends on your desire. A naked intention directed to God alone is enough.

If you want this intention summarized in a single word, in order to remember it more easily, take a short word of a single syllable. The shorter the word the better, for it will be more in tune with the work of the Spirit: a word like "God" or "love." Choose the one you like, or another you like of one syllable, and fasten this word to your heart so that it never goes away, no matter what happens.

This word will be your shield and your spear in times of peace and war alike. With this word, you will beat against the cloud and darkness above you. With this word, you will cast all thought into the cloud of forgetting. If any thoughts should press upon you and ask you what you are looking for, answer them with nothing but this single word. And if you begin to reason about the meaning and conditions of this word, simply say that you will have it whole and entire, not in bits and pieces. If you hold fast and stay true to this purpose, these thoughts will surely go away. And why? Because you will not let them feed on the sweet meditations we touched on earlier.

Entering the Cloud

- *Why does the author believe that thoughts are such a threat to the experience of God? Do they necessarily lead us away from God? Can they be used to gain a certain kind of knowledge of God? Is it possible that they may lead us to some knowledge about God rather than an actual experience of him?*

- *What is the author really interested in: knowing about God or experiencing him?*

- *Do his suggestions for dealing with distracting thoughts help?*

- *Do you have a particular word you like to use to gather in your love for God? What word or syllable have you chosen? Have you been able to use it to cast your thoughts into the cloud of forgetting?*

Chapter Eight

*A correct treatment by question and answer of certain doubts
that may arise in this work; how to deal with curiosity, cunning,
and natural intelligence; distinguishing the various degrees
and parts of the active and contemplative lives.*

Background

In this chapter, the author answers questions about the role of reason
and the experience of God and warns us against the swollen pride
of scholars and theologians. He recognizes that some thoughts can
actually increase our love and devotion for God; such thoughts
are good and can lead us along the way of holiness. He warns us,
however, that all thoughts—both good and bad—can sometimes
hinder our journey to God. To demonstrate this point, he explains
the various levels of the active and contemplative lives.

The active life has two levels: one concerned primarily with
performing the corporal works of mercy and another that unites
action with meditation and prayer. This second degree of the active
life is actually the same as the first degree of the contemplative.
He then points out that a person cannot become fully active unless he or she is at least partly contemplative. The contemplative
life, he tells us, is higher than the active. Its first degree is the
same as the second degree of the active life, where a person mixes
action together with meditative prayer. The second degree of
contemplation, however, has to do with the direct experience of
God through the cloud of unknowing. At this level, all thought is
useless; love alone will lead us through the cloud and bring us to
God. Concerned as he is with this second degree of contemplation,
he points out that even good, holy thoughts can get in the way of
our contemplative journey. For this reason, those who seek God
through the cloud must put aside all thoughts and cast them into
the cloud of forgetting.

BUT now you may ask me if that which keeps pressing upon your thoughts is good or evil. "If it were evil," you would say, "why would such thoughts increase a man's devotion so much? Sometimes, I think, it is a passing comfort to listen to such thoughts. Sometimes they move me to tears and pity for the passion of Christ or for my own inner poverty, and for many other reasons that seem holy and have done me much good. I think, therefore, that such thoughts cannot really be evil. And if they are good and have done me much good, it seems strange that you would ask me to put them away under this cloud of forgetting."

This is a very good question, and I will try to respond as best I can. First, when you ask me what it is that presses so hard upon you and offers you help in this work, I say it is a sharp and clear expression of your natural intelligence, printed in your reason within your soul. And when you ask me whether it is good or evil, I say that it must always be good in nature, since reason itself is a beam of our likeness to God. Our use of reason, however, may be good or evil. It is good, when it is enlightened by grace to help you see your own inner poverty, the passion, the kindness of God, and His wonderful works in His creation, both bodily and spiritual. It is no wonder that it would greatly increase devotion. But reason becomes evil when it becomes swollen with pride and with too much learning and book knowledge, as is the case with some clergy. It makes them strive not to be humble scholars and masters of divinity and devotion but proud scholars of the devil and masters of vanity and falsehood. In all men and women, religious or secular, the use and working of this natural intelligence is evil when it is swollen with proud and curious skills of worldly things and when it leads them to seek honors, riches, vain pleasures, and fame in this present world.

If you were to ask me why you should cast all this down into the cloud of forgetting, since it essentially good and, when used well, does you much good and increases your devotion, my response would be that there are two kinds of life in Holy Church: the active and the contemplative. The active life is the lower; the contemplative, the higher. The active life has two degrees, a higher and a lower; the contemplative also has two degrees, a higher and a lower. These two ways of life are related and, although different, depend on one another. For the higher degree of the active life is the same as the lower degree of the contemplative. A man cannot be fully active unless he is partly contemplative, nor fully contemplative (at least here on earth) without being partly active. Although the active life begins and ends in this life, the contemplative proves otherwise. It begins in this life and continues without end. The part that Mary chose will never be taken away. The active life is troubled and worries about many things; the contemplative sits peacefully with one thing.

The lower degree of the active life consists of good and honest works of mercy and charity. The higher degree of the active life (and the lower part of the contemplative life) consists of various things: spiritual meditation, knowledge of one's inner poverty, sorrow and contrition, a sympathetic and understanding consideration of Christ's passion and that of His servants, a thankful praise of God for His wonderful gifts, His kindness, and His works in His creation. But the higher degree of contemplation (at least as we presently know it) is wholly caught in this darkness and in this cloud of unknowing, with an awakened love and a blind desire for the naked being of God Himself and Him alone.

In the lower degree of the active life, a man is outside and beneath himself. In the higher degree of the active life (and the lower degree of the contemplative), a man is within himself. But in the higher degree of the contemplative life, a man is above himself and under his God. Above himself because his willful purpose is to gain by grace what he cannot attain by nature, namely, to be united to God in spirit, that is, to be one with Him in love and will. Just as it is impossible (from our perspective) for a man to practice the higher degree of the active life without stopping the lower degree for a time, so a man cannot come to the higher degree of the contemplative life without stopping the lower degree for a time. Similarly, as it would be improper and a handicap for someone engaged in meditation to consider his exterior bodily works (what he had done or ought to do, however holy those works might be), it would be just as much improper and a handicap for a man who should be working in divine darkness—and in this cloud of unknowing, whose love is moving out to God Himself—to allow any thought or meditation of God's wonderful gifts, or kindness, or any of His created works, physical or spiritual, to be placed between him and his God, however pleasant or inspiring those thoughts may be.

For this reason, I ask you to put down these sharp, tenuous thoughts and cover them with a thick cloud of forgetting, even when they are holy and promise to achieve their goal. Why? Because love may reach up to God, even in this life, but not knowledge. While the soul dwells in this mortal body, the keenness of our spiritual understanding, especially of God, is dulled and causes our actions to be imperfect. Apart from God's grace, these actions would lead us into much error.

Entering the Cloud

- *Do you agree that even good thoughts can sometimes get in the way of our journey to God? Have you ever had such an experience?*

- *What degree of the active or contemplative life are you presently living?*

- *Do you feel called to the active or contemplative life?*

- *Do you believe the contemplative life is higher than the active?*

- *Do you understand how active and contemplative lives overlap?*

- *Do you agree that the purely contemplative life takes a person beyond all thought and into a direct experience of the divine?*

Chapter Nine

*During this work, recalling the holiest creature ever made
by God is an impediment rather than a help.*

Background

In this chapter, the author tells us that in order to penetrate the cloud of unknowing we must suppress our desire to know through all words and concepts. If we do not put them down, even the holiest of thoughts will ultimately prevent us from achieving our heart's desire. Nothing must stand between us and God, not even thought itself. Whenever we find ourselves in this dark, impenetrable cloud, we must struggle against our thoughts and hold in check our understanding and desire to know. Love alone will lead us to God, and this divine impulse depends on God's grace and nothing else. The author reminds us that we can penetrate the cloud only by being persistent in responding to this divine inspiration until we ultimately break through its seemingly impenetrable wall and experience God directly. To do this, we must keep the eyes of our souls open at all times and be on guard against all that might lead us astray. Doing so is more important than all other endeavors in the spiritual life, for it allows God to draw our love for him up into the cloud of unknowing and ultimately beyond it. The author is not saying that thought is evil or that it does not have a designated purpose. He is only pointing out that it has no place in the way of pure contemplation and that, if we wish to know God perfectly, we must follow the inspirations of divine love and not those of human knowledge.

TEXT

THEREFORE, the intense activity of your mind, which will always press upon you when you begin this work, must always be suppressed. Unless you do so, it will weigh you down. Often enough, when you think you are in this darkness and that nothing is in your mind but God, if you look carefully you will find your mind not occupied with this darkness but with something less than God. And if this be so, then that thing can be said to be momentarily above you and between you and God. As holy and attractive as these reflections may seem, make up your mind to suppress them. For I tell you, it is more beneficial for the health of your soul, more worthwhile, and more pleasing to God and to all the saints and angels in heaven—more helpful to all your friends, bodily and spiritual, living and dead—that you have this blind stirring of love for God Himself in your spiritual affection, this secret pressing upon this cloud of unknowing, than to have the eyes of your soul opened in contemplation, or to behold all the angels or saints, or to hear all their mirth and happy music in heaven.

Do not be surprised by this. See it but once (and by grace you can), get hold of it and feel it and you will always see it. Know, however, that you will never have an unclouded vision of God in this life, although you may have an awareness of Him, if He grants you the grace for it. So lift up your love to that cloud. To be more precise, let God lift your love into that cloud and strive by His grace to forget everything else.

For if any naked thought comes up against your will and puts you further from God than you should be (insofar as it makes you less able to experience the fruit of His love), how much more upsetting will a thought be that is deliberately entertained and nourished? And since a thought of any special saint or of any good and holy spiritual thing will hinder your spiritual growth when you are engaged in this contemplative activity, how much more will the thought of any other living person or any other physical or worldly thing?

I am not saying that the sudden, unanticipated thought of something good and holy that commands your mind's and will's attention or a thought that you have deliberately called forth to deepen your devotion is necessarily evil, even though it may prove to be an obstacle. God forbid that you should understand me in this way. But I do say that for all its goodness and holiness, whenever someone seeks to contemplate God, it is more of a hindrance than a help. Surely whoever seeks God in pure contemplation will not find rest in merely meditating on the angels and saints in heaven.

Entering the Cloud

- *What is it about the nature of thought that prevents us from experiencing God directly?*

- *How do you think the author would respond to those who insist that the mystical experience of God takes place first and foremost in the intellect?*

- *Can you see the difference between a word or thought that comes to mind and the reality it is trying to express? Is the author trying to say something similar about mystical experience?*

- *What is it about love that leads us to God? What enables it to penetrate what thought cannot? Can love coexist with thought?*

- *If God is the ultimate source of all thought, why is he also beyond it?*

- *Does anything lie beyond pure love?*

Chapter Ten

How to know whether a thought is sinful and, if it be sinful, whether it is mortal or venial.

Background

In this chapter, the author gives us some insight into the nature of temptation. He does so by looking more deeply into the nature of thought and telling us how to discern whether the ideas that come to us are evil and whether they are light or serious. Even the simplest idea, he tells us, may not be sinful, but it is still beyond our control and should be seen as an effect of original sin. Because we were cleansed from this sin of human nature at baptism, we have the capacity through the influence of divine grace to bat it down and prevent it from influencing our hearts. If not dealt with immediately, such thoughts can lead to sinful desires, which can be very serious (even deadly) for those who live in the world.

This same affection is less serious for those who have forsaken the world and seek to live the contemplative life. But if those who have chosen the contemplative life allow such sinful thoughts and affections to remain, they are in danger of regressing in the spiritual life. If they not only allow them to remain, but also freely assent to them, these thoughts and affections will penetrate their fleshly hearts and influence their spiritual hearts. When this happens, such thoughts and affections become deadly and give rise to the capital sins of wrath, envy, sloth, pride, covetousness, gluttony, and lust. The author remains firm in his insistence that thought cannot bring us to God and can, in fact, ultimately be responsible for our spiritual demise.

BUT it is not so with any and every recollection of any living person or thing. For a sudden thought that enters your mind without previous desire or forethought cannot be sinful. Although it may be sinful in the sense that it is an effect of original sin, through which you lost control over your thoughts, you were cleansed from the guilt of that sin at baptism. It can only become sinful if this sudden urge is not quickly put down, because otherwise you will be immediately attracted to it. It may be something you like—a thing that pleases you or has pleased you in the past—or it may be something that grieves you or has grieved you before. To those already living in mortal sin, this attention may be mortally sinful. But to you and all others who have forsaken the world and live devoutly in obedience to Holy Church (whether privately or publicly) and who intend to be governed not by your own will or knowledge but by that of your superiors, religious or secular, this natural attraction or complaint is nothing more than a venial sin. The reason is that your intention when you first entered the contemplative state in which you now stand (with the knowledge and sense of a prudent spiritual father) was rooted and grounded in God.

But if you make room for this thing that you naturally like or dislike and make no attempt to rebuke it, it will ultimately take root in your inmost being with your full consent. Then for you it is a deadly sin. This happens whenever you, or any of those I have been speaking of, deliberately call someone or something to mind. If it is something that injures or has injured you, then you are filled with rage and want revenge—and that is *Wrath*. Or you will look upon it with contempt and hate it and think spitefully and harshly of it—and that is *Envy*. Or you will get tired and bored with being good in spirit and body—and that is *Sloth*.

And if it is something pleasing, present or past, you experience a temporary delight when you think about it, whatever it may be. You dwell on it and in the end fix your heart and will on it and turn to it for nourishment. At such times, you think that you want only to live in peace and quiet with this pleasant thing. Now, if this thought that you deliberately call upon, or harbor, and dwell upon lovingly, is natural worth or knowledge, charm or station, favor or beauty, then it is *Pride*. If it pertains to material goods, riches or possessions, ownership or lordship, then it is *Avarice*. If it is a matter of choice food and drink or any other delight of the palate, then it is *Gluttony*. If it is love or pleasure or any manner of flirting, fawning, and flattering—for another or for yourself— then it is *Lust*.

Entering the Cloud

- *Do you agree with the author's presentation of temptation? Do you agree with him that it comes from thoughts (even simple and innocent ones) that can lead to sinful desires? Do you agree that such thoughts must be suppressed immediately, lest they get out of control and lead to the assent of the will?*

- *How do you determine which thoughts may lead to sinful desires? When the thought itself appears? When the evil desires first arise? Have you ever thought about where the thoughts you get throughout the day come from?*

- *Have you ever sensed a need to monitor your thoughts and guard against those that may be harmful to your spiritual well-being?*

Chapter Eleven

*A person should weigh each thought and impulse for what it is
and always avoid carelessness in venial sin.*

Background

In this chapter, the author emphasizes the importance of monitoring
our thoughts so that they do not lead us into sin. He cautions us
against being careless about the danger they pose. Every thought
and impulse must be taken seriously and given its due. Those of
us who are indifferent to them will eventually become victim to
them. At the very least, such thoughts and impulses will lead us
into venial sin. The author reminds us that, although it is impossible to be free of such sins in the present life, those wishing to
enter the state of pure contemplation must do all it takes to avoid
them. The path of true discipleship abhors sin of every kind. Lack
of care regarding venial sins can easily lead into the realm of deadly
sin. For this reason, we must be ever ready to examine carefully
all of our thoughts and desires. There is no other way to separate
the chaff from the wheat.

TEXT

I SAY this not because I think that you, or any others of whom I
speak, are guilty and encumbered by such sins but because I want
you to weigh each thought as it arises and work hard to destroy
the first stirring of anything that might lead you into sin. For I can
tell you this: The one who does not weigh, or who underestimates,
the first thought—even if it be not sinful—will not avoid carelessness when it comes to venial sin. No one can avoid committing
venial sin in this life, but all true disciples of holiness should not
be careless regarding them. Otherwise, I would not be surprised
if they eventually led to deadly sin.

Entering the Cloud

- *Do you see the importance of scrutinizing your thoughts and the desires they spawn?*

- *Does such watchfulness come naturally or must it be acquired over time through daily practice?*

- *Does grace play a role in developing such a disposition? Is it something we can ask God for?*

- *Do you examine your thoughts and desires? Do you do so regularly or only sporadically?*

- *Can you think of any concrete steps or practices that might help to root such watchfulness more deeply in your heart? Could it simply be a matter of recognizing your limitations and asking God for help?*

Chapter Twelve

Through this work, sin is destroyed and virtues are acquired.

Background

In this chapter, the author encourages us to beat against the dark, impermeable cloud of unknowing again and again with the sharpened and pointed dart of love. This impulse of love has its origins in God. It will not only root out sin in our lives but also lead us along the way of virtue. For this intense impulse of love to take effect, however, we must cast out of our minds all things but God himself. Only the cloud of unknowing should stand between us and our heart's desire. In time, even that will dissipate, and we will experience the divine reality in all its fullness. Nothing but this intense desire and love for God will lead us to God. No other ascetical practice, however strict and rigorous, will dig out the roots of sin from our lives or instill in us the dispositions of a virtuous soul. Without this blind impulse of love, whatever virtues we actually acquire will never be complete. There will always be something askew in their capacity to inspire us to do good.

The author defines virtue as "an ordered and measured affection plainly directed to God himself." He reminds us that God alone enables us to be virtuous and that what we do is merely cooperate with his grace. If we have any other motive in becoming virtuous than God himself, then whatever virtue we do attain will be lacking in perfection. Humility and charity are the key virtues. To possess one is to possess them all.

TEXT

AND so if you desire to stand and not fall, never stray from your purpose but beat relentlessly on this cloud of unknowing between you and God. Do so with a sharp dart of longing love and avoid thinking of anything else but God, no matter what happens. This alone will destroy the ground and root of sin. Regardless of how long you fast, keep vigil, rise early, harden your bed, make coarse your hairshirt, and—if it were permitted (which it is not)—put out your eyes, cut your tongue from your mouth, plug up your ears and nose, cut off your limbs, yes, discipline your body in every way imaginable, all this would amount to nothing. For the tendency and movement toward sin would still be in you.

Yes, and what is more, if you constantly wept in sorrow for your sins and Christ's Passion or pondered without ceasing the joys of heaven, what good would it do you? It would certainly gain you much good, much help, much profit, and much grace. In comparison with this blind stirring of love, however, it does or will do very little. This contemplative mindset is the best part chosen by Mary.[11] Without it, all these other things amount to little. It destroys not only the ground and root of sin but also nourishes virtue. For if it is authentic, all the virtues shall be truly and perfectly conceived and understood, without any other intent. Without it, a person can never possess so many virtues, for they are usually mingled with some crooked intent by which they become imperfect.

For virtue is nothing more than an ordered and measured affection plainly directed to God Himself. And why? God alone is the pure cause of all virtues. If anyone is stirred to any one virtue by any mixed motivation, even though God is still foremost, then his virtue is imperfect. This is evident especially in the case of humility and charity. For whoever possesses these virtues needs no others, for he possesses everything.

Entering the Cloud

- *Do you agree that the love of God, and the love of God alone, will root out sin from your life and make you virtuous?*

- *Do you agree that, without it, all the ascetical practices you do will fall short of leading you to perfection?*

- *Do you agree with the author's description of virtue? Does he overlook anything important or include something that should be omitted?*

- *Why does the author emphasize so much the virtues of humility and charity? Do you agree that they open the way to possessing the other virtues? Do you find them lacking in your life? If so, to what extent?*

- *What can you do to become more humble and charitable in your daily life?*

Chapter Thirteen

What is perfect humility? What is imperfect humility?

Background

In this chapter, the author gives us more insight into the nature of humility. He tells us that humility has to do with knowing ourselves as we truly are in the sight of God. There are two kinds of humility: perfect and imperfect. The first is very difficult (but not impossible) to attain in this life, since it has God as its one and only source and object. We are likely to have only brief glimpses of it at certain unique, grace-filled moments in our lives. At such times, we lose awareness of our smallness and sinfulness before God and stand in complete awe of his glorious and powerful presence. We would be entirely overwhelmed by this presence if God in his infinite wisdom did not ensure that our experience of him was proportionate to what we are capable of receiving. He does not wish to overpower us with his presence, but he meets us where we are and reveals himself accordingly.

Imperfect humility, by way of contrast, introduces other motives and intentions into our humble self-awareness before God. Such humility is much more common in this life. It is rooted not only in God but also in other desires and worldly objects. This tainted mixture of motives can easily be infected with pride and other self-centered tendencies. Because it is still tied to this world, this kind of humility will disappear at the end of our earthly sojourn. It should not be mistaken for its perfect, purified counterpart, which is rooted solely in God and lasts forever.

TEXT

LET us first consider humility. It is imperfect when it stems from mixed motivations—even if God is the main motive—and perfect when caused by God alone. If we are to understand it properly, we must first know what humility is. Then we may be able to determine its cause with more accuracy.

In itself, humility is nothing but a true knowledge and experience of oneself as one truly is. For whoever sees and experiences himself as he is would truly be humble. Humility comes from two sources. One is the filth, wretchedness, and frailty of man into which he has fallen through sin and which he always feels to some extent in this life, regardless of how holy he is. The other is the superabundant love and worthiness of God Himself, before whom all of nature quakes, all scholars are fools, and all saints and angels are blind. To be sure, had He not through His divine wisdom measured their vision of Himself according to their capacity in nature and grace, I cannot say what would have happened to them.

This second cause is perfect because it is eternal. The first is imperfect because it is temporal and because it often happens that a soul living in this mortal body may suddenly lose and forget all awareness and sense of its own being and take no account of its holiness or wretchedness. This happens through the movement of grace that deepens its longing for as often and as long as God allows it. But does this happen to a soul thus disposed often or seldom? I believe it lasts but for a short while and that in this time it is perfectly humble, for it knows and feels no cause but the principal one: God Himself. But when it knows and feels another cause, even if God Himself remains primary, its humility is still imperfect. Nevertheless, even this humility is good and should be experienced. God forbid that you understand this in any other way.

Entering the Cloud

- *Do you agree with the author's description of humility? Do you see any difficulties in his distinction between perfect and imperfect humility?*

- *What do you think about his assertion that perfect humility is very difficult to attain in this life? Does it make sense to you? Is it something you can attain without God's help?*

- *Do you consider yourself a humble person? Do others see you that way? Do you want to be viewed that way?*

- *What are your motives for wanting to be humble?*

Chapter Fourteen

Without imperfect humility, it is impossible for a sinner to attain perfect humility in this life.

Background

In this chapter, the author emphasizes the importance of imperfect humility for this life. Even though it falls short of perfection, it has a number of benefits. For one thing, it provides us with an authentic (albeit limited) knowledge of ourselves before God and thus puts us on the path to perfect humility. It also has the capacity to lead us along this way fairly quickly, since possessing it, in his mind, is more effective than the prayers of all the angels, saints, and living faithful combined. Because we are sinners, the author tells us that it is virtually impossible for us to become perfectly humble without first experiencing this imperfect form of the virtue. He therefore encourages us to work diligently to gain a true knowledge of ourselves before God in the midst of our mixed motivations and intentions. If we do so, he believes that we will gradually come to the point where we experience God as he truly is.

This experience will not represent God's own experience of himself or the experience we will have of him in heaven but only what is possible for us in the present life. Fleeting as it may be, it points to what is in store for us in the life to come. The author does not want to give the impression that he wants us to stop striving for imperfect humility. He tells us about its elusive counterpart not to discourage us but to give us a deeper sense of the virtue's true origin in God. He also wishes to correct any false impressions we might have about the kind of humility we presently possess. His goal in all this is to make us more humble than we presently are. He does not want us to deceive ourselves into thinking we are truly humble when, in fact, we possess only a pale reflection of the completed virtue. He wants us to value imperfect humility and see it as a way of working toward gaining the perfection of the virtue.

TEXT

EVEN though I call it imperfect humility, I would much rather have a true knowledge and awareness of myself as I am. And I believe that this knowledge and awareness would help me arrive at perfect humility sooner than if all the saints and angels in heaven and all the men and women of the Holy Church living on earth—religious or seculars of all states—were to gather together and do nothing but pray to God for me to receive perfect humility. Indeed, it is impossible for a sinner to get hold of and retain perfect humility without imperfect humility.

Therefore, do all you can and may do to get a true knowledge and awareness of yourself as you are. I believe that, soon after doing so, you will have a true knowledge and awareness of God as He is. Not as He is in Himself, for that no one can have but God Himself. And not as you will have in heaven with both body and soul together. But, as God permits, as much as it is now possible for a humble soul in a mortal body to know and experience Him.

And do not think that, because I have marked out two causes of humility, one perfect and another imperfect, I want you to forsake the hard work of imperfect humility and focus entirely on perfect humility. Certainly not! May it not be so! Rather, you should see the importance of this spiritual exercise over all other physical or spiritual exercises even when these are done under the influence of grace. The secret love of a purified soul, pressing continually upon this dark cloud of unknowing between you and God, contains perfect humility within itself without seeking anything other than God. I say this because I want you to arrive at perfect humility and prepare your heart to love, for your sake and mine, and because I want this knowledge of yourself to make you even more humble.

For a lack of knowledge is often the cause of great pride. What is more, in all likelihood, if you did not know what perfect humility was, you would think that, when you had a little knowledge and experience of imperfect humility, you had nearly arrived at perfect humility. And so you would deceive yourself into thinking you were perfectly humble when all the while you were full of foul and stinking pride. Therefore, try to work for perfect humility. Its nature is such that, whoever possesses it does not sin for as long as he has it—and not much afterward.

Entering the Cloud

- *Do you agree with the author's assessment of imperfect humility? Do you see how it can be of help to you in your spiritual journey? Do you believe that it can prepare you for and eventually lead you to perfect humility?*

- *Do you believe you can get a taste of perfect humility in the present life? Have you tasted it before?*

- *Where would you place yourself on the path to perfect humility? Utterly lost? Just starting out? Somewhere along the way? Nearing the end?*

- *Has the author's presentation increased your appreciation of the importance of humility for Christian discipleship? Has it deepened your desire to be truly humble?*

Chapter Fifteen

A brief rebuttal of the error that says there is no better way of becoming humble than through the knowledge of one's own sinfulness.

Background

In this chapter, the author encourages us to strive for perfect humility and to live in hope of attaining it in this life. He deals with the common misperception that the best way of becoming truly humble in the present life is to be constantly aware of our wretchedness and sinfulness before God. Although such an approach may help us along the way of humility, it is ultimately incomplete. Useful to habitual sinners (like himself, he is quick to point out), it is less effective for those who have progressed in holiness and lead relatively innocent, sinless lives. It also fails to take into account the perfect humility of Christ and our Blessed Mother, who lived their earthly sojourn without ever sinning. Nor does it correspond to the experience of the angels and saints who, influenced by God's benevolent grace, have been able to live without sin and gain possession of the completed virtue. For this reason, the author tells us that the best way to strive for perfect humility is to be aware of its first and only cause: the gratuitous gift of God's grace. He reminds us that grace alone is the ultimate cause of perfect humility. For this reason, the best way to attain this virtue is to be aware of its true cause and to constantly ask for God's grace to become perfectly meek and humble.

TEXT

YOU must trust me when I say that there is perfect humility and that it comes to us in this life through God's grace. I say this to refute the error that says that there is no better cause of perfect humility than the remembrance of our wretchedness and our past sins.

I certainly admit that for those, like myself, who have been habitual sinners, it is both necessary and effective to be humbled under the remembrance of our wretchedness and past sins, until the time when our conscience and counsel avow that the great rust of sin has in large part been rubbed away. But to those who have not sinned mortally, habitually, or deliberately but only through frailty and ignorance and who desire to be contemplatives—and to us too, if our director and our conscience agree that we have lawfully amended our lives through contrition, confession, and penance, after the statutes and ordinances of the Holy Church, and especially if we feel moved by grace to become contemplatives—there is another way of becoming humble. That way is far above the imperfect cause spoken of earlier. It is the life of our Lady, St. Mary. Hers is above the life of the most sinful penitent in Holy Church, or as the life of Christ is above the life of any man who ever lived, or as the life of any angel in heaven, who has never known or will ever feel frailty, is above the life of the weakest man on earth.

If there is no perfect cause to make us humble, but only the knowledge of our own wretchedness, then I would ask those who hold such an opinion, what is it that humbles those—such as Our Lord Jesus Christ, Our Lady St. Mary, and all the saints and angels in heaven—who do not know the wretchedness of sin? In the Gospel, Our Lord Jesus Christ Himself calls us to this and other perfections when He bids to be perfect by grace, as He is by nature. [12]

Entering the Cloud

- *Do you believe it is possible for you to become perfectly humble (if only for a time) even in this present life?*

- *Do you agree with the author that consciousness of your wretchedness and sinfulness before God must be complemented by awareness of the virtue's primary cause and then asking for the grace to become truly humble?*

- *Does this approach make sense to you? Have you used it in the past?*

- *Do you think the author's approach is worth trying? Is it merely a matter of saying something like, "Lord, give me the grace to become truly humble?"*

Chapter Sixteen

Through this work, a sinner who is truly converted and called to contemplation reaches perfection sooner than through any other means and quickly receives from God forgiveness of his sins.

Background

In this chapter, the author tells us not to allow our sinful and broken humanity to get in the way of our quiet knocking on the cloud of unknowing with the humble impulse of love. He points to Mary, a previously sinful woman, as an example of someone called to the contemplative life. [13] Conscious of her deep sinfulness and utter unworthiness before God, she was even more mindful of her lack of love for her Lord. The author recognizes the help that an awareness of our past sins can give us in becoming truly humble and, for this reason, encourages us to have deep sorrow for our past sins and to weep bitterly for them as Mary did. At the same time, he tells us that it is useless and possibly even harmful for us to focus exclusively on our past sins by digging them up and mourning over them one by one. He encourages us instead to take advantage of the ordinary ways of making amendment for our sins and then simply to carry them all quietly in a secret place in our hearts, where they will continue to remind us of our unworthiness of God's love. This is what Mary did, and the author encourages us to do the same.

Instead of being consumed by our past sins, it is much more important for us to be mournful and sorrowful for our lack of love for God. This deep mourning and inner sighing for our inability to love God is characteristic of the true lover. He points out that someone who truly loves God will always long to love him more deeply. The author points out the danger of concentrating on the sins of the past to the exclusion of our longing and love for God. He encourages us to follow Mary's example by hanging our lack of love and our longing for God on the cloud of unknowing. Doing so will deepen our love for God and help us to be more and more absorbed by his love for us.

TEXT

NO ONE need presume that he, the most wretched sinner in the world, after true amendment and a subsequent call to contemplation, and with the consent of his director and his conscience, now dares to offer God his humble love and press into that cloud of unknowing between him and God. For our Lord said to Mary Magdalene, the representative of all sinners called to contemplative life, "Your sins are forgiven." He did so not because of her great sorrow or because of her remembrance of her sins or because of her humility as she beheld her wretchedness, but because she loved much.

Here we can see what secret and insistent love can obtain from our Lord: far beyond anything we could imagine. Still, I grant that she was deeply sorrowful, wept for her sins, and was greatly humbled by the thought of her wretchedness. We, too, who have been wretched and habitual sinners, must also be full of fearful and awful sorrow for our sins and deeply humbled in our remembrance of our wretchedness.

But how? Surely as Mary did. Although she might not always have felt a deep heartfelt sorrow of her sins all her life, she carried them with her wherever she went as a burden bound together and laid up secretly in the depths of her heart, in a manner never to be forgotten. Nevertheless, Scripture affirms that she had more heartfelt sorrow, more doleful longing, more deep sighing, and more intense and almost fatal languishing for her lack of love, even though she already had great love. Do not be surprised by this, for the more a true lover loves, the more she longs to love.

And yet she knew very well and felt in her heart that she was the most foul and wretched of sinners and that her sins had caused the distance between her and the God she loved so much, and that they were the main cause of her languishing weakness for lack of love. What of it? Did she descend from the heights of her longing to the depths of her sinful life to search in the foul stinking fen and dunghill of her sins, calling them up one by one, with all their circumstances, and sorrowing and weeping over each in turn? Of course not! And why? Because God let her know by His grace in her soul that she could never bring it about in this way. If she had done this, it was far more likely that she would begin sinning again, than to simply to seek forgiveness for all her sins.

And therefore she hung up her love and her longing desire in this cloud of unknowing and learned to love what in this life she might not clearly understand by the light of reason nor delight in with her affections. And she loves Him so that she often has little recollection of ever being a sinner at all. Yes, and I often think that she was so deeply disposed to the love of His Godhead that she gave little thought to the beauty of His precious and blessed body as He sat and spoke and preached to her, nor for that matter, to anything else physical or spiritual. This seems to be the Gospel teaching.

Entering the Cloud

- *How much are you bothered by your sinful past? How much do you mourn it and express your sorrow for it? Does it come to mind often or at all? Do you carry it with you throughout the day on the periphery of your awareness?*

- *Do you concentrate too much on your past sins? Which do you mourn more, your sinfulness or your lack of love for God?*

- *Do you agree with the author that mourning your lack of love for God is more important than mourning your sinful past?*

- *Like Mary, do you bring your lack of love for God and your longing to love him more to prayer? Are you able to hang them both on the cloud of unknowing?*

- *Do you in any way allow the awareness of your sinfulness get in the way of your love for God?*

Chapter Seventeen

A true contemplative does not concern himself with the
active life or with what is done or spoken about him;
nor should he respond to his accusers.

Background

In this chapter, the author explores more deeply Martha and Mary's relationship to Jesus and uses it as a metaphor for the active and contemplative lives. He tells us that Martha, who upon the Lord's visit to her home busies herself with the duties of household hospitality, is the model par excellence of the active life. He identifies her specifically with the first stage of the active life, which focuses on the corporal acts of mercy more than the meditations and devotions common to the second state of active life and the first stage of the contemplative. Her sister, Mary, by way of contrast, is the model par excellence of the purely contemplative life. She is someone who has received the call to contemplation and has responded positively to the grace necessary for it. At this deep level of contemplative living, she is not at all concerned with activities like waiting on the Lord like her sister, Martha. Even though such activities are good and holy in themselves, Mary is not called to perform them at this stage of her contemplative journey. She is instead being called to simply sit beside the Lord, rest in his presence, and allow her love for him to come to the fore.

The author goes on to say that Mary is so caught up in the Lord's divine presence that she is not absorbed in the Lord's human life and earthly ministry, a characteristic more common to the second stage of the active life and the first stage of the contemplative. Instead, she has been called to cease all outward activity and simply gaze with love upon the cloud of unknowing until the Lord draws her completely into his divine presence through the gentle movements of his grace. He also points out that those in the active life (especially those in the first stage) will not understand such inactivity and will complain to the Lord, as Martha does, about this seeming insensitivity. He goes on to say that, like Mary, those in the second stage of contemplation should not try to explain themselves against such accusations or defend themselves in any way. Absorbed in the contemplation of the divine presence, they have no leisure to listen to or answer such complaints. Attempting to do so would do nothing but turn them away from their call and lead them away from the cloud of unknowing rather than into and ultimately beyond it.

TEXT

THE GOSPEL of Luke says that when our Lord was in the house of Martha, her sister, Mary, sat at His feet, while Martha busied herself preparing His meal. [14] While listening to Him, Mary did not share in her sister's work, although this activity was entirely good and holy since it is the first part of the active life. Nor did she concern herself with the Lord's physical appearance or His kind voice and compassionate words, although this was even better and holier since it is the second part of the active life and the first of the contemplative.

But she beheld with all her heart the supreme wisdom of His Godhead lapped in the dark words of His humanity. Nothing she saw or heard could budge her, but there she sat, completely still, with deep delight and an ardent love pressed upon that high cloud of unknowing between her and God. For I tell you this: There is no creature in this life, nor ever shall be, so highly ravished in contemplation and love of the Godhead that there is not a high and a wonderful cloud of unknowing between him and God. It was in this cloud that Mary experienced the many secret movements of her love. And why? Because it was the best and the holiest part of contemplation there can be in this life, and from this experience nothing on earth could move her. So much so that when her sister, Martha, complained about her to our Lord and bade Him to tell her sister to rise and help her and let her not do so much work by herself, she remained completely still and answered with not a single word nor showed as much as a grumbling gesture against her sister for any of her complaints. And no wonder! She had another work to do that Martha did not understand. And so she had no time to listen to her and answer her complaint.

My friend, all these works, words, and gestures shared by our Lord and these two sisters are an example of all actives and contemplatives who have arisen in Holy Church from that time until the day of judgment. By Mary is understood all contemplatives, who should conform their lives after hers. And by Martha, all actives, who should do likewise and for the same reason.

Entering the Cloud

- *Do you accept the author's basic comparison of Martha and Mary as representative of active and contemplative lives?*
- *Do you agree with his further interpretation that, according to the stages of the spiritual life, Martha stands for someone in the first stage of the active life (that is, someone concerned solely with performing good and holy works), while her sister, Mary, stands for someone in the second stage of the contemplative (that is, someone concerned solely with contemplating the divine presence)?*
- *Does any part of his presentation seem to you unusual or a bit forced?*
- *Are you aware of any other interpretations connecting Martha and Mary to active and contemplative lives?*
- *What do the historical exegetes of today have to say about it?*
- *Do you consider yourself an active, a contemplative, or a bit of both?*
- *Do you think God is calling you to live more like Martha or Mary?*
- *Is he calling you to lead a life of pure action or pure contemplation? In this life or the next?*

Chapter Eighteen

Actives complain about contemplatives, as Martha did of Mary.
Ignorance is the cause of these complaints.

Background

In this chapter, the author looks into why those in the active life complain so much about those who feel called to forsake all outward activity and focus their energies instead on a life of pure contemplation. He points out that those in the active life, whether they are lay or religious, generally respond negatively to those who have discerned a calling to a life of pure contemplation. He tells us that this occurs even when this discernment has taken place under the guidance of one's conscience and with the help of a spiritual director. Those not familiar with the movement and inner working of God's grace in a person's heart will not understand the meaning of such a radical break from all outward activity. Even the contemplative's family and closest friends will find reasons (some seemingly very good ones) for him or her to do otherwise. In addition to pointing out the wastefulness of such inactivity, they will point out the many examples of others who have set out on this dark, lonely path and have ended up worse than when they started off. Many will become hypocritical in their living the life of Christian discipleship and, in some cases, may even end up in the service of the evil one. The author acknowledges these very real dangers and promises to deal with them at a later point. For the moment, he wishes to concentrate on the authenticity of the call to the contemplative life and to remind us that, for the most part, the complaints of actives against contemplatives stem from ignorance and a lack of understanding of their unique call within the Church.

TEXT

JUST as Martha complained about her sister, Mary, so to this day do all actives complain about contemplatives. For it happens that people from any state in life, whatever kind it may be, religious or secular—without exception—feel moved by grace and counsel to forsake all outward activity and to go about living the contemplative life according to their ability, conscience, and spiritual counsel. Very soon afterward, however, their own brothers and sisters and close friends, along with many others who know nothing of their desires or the manner of life they wish to live, set upon them with many complaints and tell them they should not do it. And they will quickly tell them all sorts of tales, some false and some true, of men and women who have given themselves to such a life and fallen. And there is never a tale about those who have persevered.

I admit that many of those who seem to have forsaken the world fall and have fallen. Because they would not follow true spiritual counsel, they became the devil's servants and his contemplatives, turning into hypocrites or heretics and falling into frenzies and much other mischief in slander of Holy Church, when they should have become God's servants and His contemplatives. I will not speak of these fallen contemplatives at this time, for it would lead us far afield. I will later on, if God allows and, if need be, we may examine the conditions and cause of their failings. But no more of them at this time, for we must look to our present concerns.

Entering the Cloud

- *Have you ever seen those in the active life complain about the attitudes and lifestyle of those in the contemplative life? If so, what kinds of things do they say? Are they true? Are they rooted in a lack of understanding? Are they perhaps rooted in a mixture of both?*

- *Have you ever shared in such complaints? If so, were you on the giving or receiving end? Were you complaining from the active side or listening from the contemplative?*

- *Do you recognize the dangers in store for someone who sets out to live a life of pure contemplation but is not really called to it?*

- *To what extent is the author trying to raise an awareness of these dangers in the minds of his readers?*

- *To what extent is he trying to help them focus on the true nature of the call to contemplation?*

Chapter Nineteen

The author's brief explanation of why all contemplatives should excuse actives completely for their complaining words and deeds.

Background

In this chapter, the author explains his motivations for drawing out the complaints of actives against contemplatives. He tells us that he does not in any way mean to dishonor Martha and the life of active service she represents. He acknowledges her great holiness and tells us that we must be ready to understand and even make excuses for whatever criticisms she might have concerning the contemplative calling of her sister. He points out, moreover, that Martha reveals her concerns about her sister directly to the Lord and does so in a few words and with great courtesy. He asks us to interpret these sincere words in their proper context, accept that she is simply speaking from a lack of knowledge of the contemplative way, and make every possible excuse for her. Although incorrect and misdirected, her words are to be viewed more as an attempt at sisterly correction than a scathing indictment of the contemplative journey.

The author goes on to say that we should strive to make similar excuses for everyone else in the active life who makes similar statements about the contemplative life from their lack of knowledge and understanding. He also tells us that we should do so even when their words appear more biting than those of Martha. Since the active life is the only path of Christian discipleship they understand, we should interpret their criticisms of the contemplative as a veiled attempt of defending and honoring their own way of life. The author also says that we should be willing to forgive the faults of others done in ignorance, since God himself has done the same for us. If he has been so merciful and forgiving toward us for the faults we have committed out of ignorance, should we not do the same for others?

Text

SOME may think that I am paying little respect to Martha, that special saint, in comparing her complaints to those of worldly men, or theirs with hers. I can only say that I mean no disrespect to her or to them. God forbid that I should say anything in this book that might in any way be taken as a condemnation of any of the servants of God, particularly of this special saint. I think we can excuse her complaint by taking into account the time and manner in which she said it. She said what she said without knowing the cause. No wonder she did not know how her sister, Mary, was occupied at the time. For I think she had previously heard very little of such perfection. And since her words were courteous and few, we must excuse her completely.

I think that the men and women who live the active life should also be completely excused of their complaints, even though they say it rudely, since they, too, are ignorant. And why? Just as Martha knew very little about what her sister, Mary, was doing when she complained to our Lord, in the same manner these folk nowadays know little or nothing of what these young disciples of God mean when they set themselves apart from the activity of the world and seek to be God's special servants in holiness and righteousness. And if they knew, I daresay they would neither do nor say what they did. Therefore, I think they should always be excused, since they know no better life than the one they are living. Also, when I think of my own innumerable faults done out of ignorance, I think I should be charitable and merciful toward the ignorant words and deeds of others and always excuse them, if I wish to be forgiven by God for my own. Otherwise, I am not doing unto others as I would have them do unto me.

Entering the Cloud

- *Do you agree with the author that contemplatives should make every excuse for those who criticize their way of life out of ignorance and a lack of understanding?*

- *Do you agree that they should not defend themselves against such criticisms because doing so would be a distraction that might lead them away from the path of contemplation?*

- *Do you think contemplatives should remain silent and not defend themselves even when the criticisms of their way of life are carefully planned and well-thought-out?*

- *As someone seeking to live a contemplative life, do you think you could remain silent in the face of such criticisms?*

- *If you were Mary and had overheard your sister making such comments to the Lord, would you be able to keep your composure and resist responding? Would you need God's help to do so? Would you be able to ask for it?*

Chapter Twenty

How Almighty God will answer for all who do not wish to leave their activity of loving of Him in order to defend themselves.

Background

In this chapter, the author tells contemplatives not to be concerned with the complaints of others but to focus instead on resting in the divine presence. This is the sole task set before them. They should leave the complaints of others to God, just as Mary remained silent and allowed Jesus to take up Martha's complaint. Rather than judging her and asking her to help her sister, Jesus recognizes Mary's deep love for him and understands what lies behind her contemplative longing. By telling Martha that she is much occupied and that her sister, Mary, has chosen the best part, he reminds us that, in the end, there is only one thing that matters—to love the Lord our God with all our hearts. Rather than judging Mary, he thus becomes her staunch defender. He does so, however, not by denigrating Martha's vocation to the active life but simply by pointing out that the very nature of her call involves being troubled about many things for the sake of others.

While reminding us of the nobility of the purely active life, Jesus' words also make it clear that such a life (even when mixed with the contemplative) ultimately falls short in its love for God. Martha's love is incomplete because it focuses on things other than God; Mary's love is complete because it does nothing but render praise, honor, and glory to God alone. Martha's love will disappear unless it develops into Mary's. Mary's love, by way of contrast, will continue in this life and reach its fruition in the next, when it will become completely one with God.

TEXT

THEREFORE, I think those who set out to be contemplatives should not only excuse actives of their complaints but also be so immersed in the spiritual things that they take little heed of what others say or do concerning them. Mary, our example in all this, did just that when her sister, Martha, complained to our Lord. If we do likewise, our Lord will do for us now what He did then for Mary.

And what was that? Surely this: our loving Lord Jesus Christ, from whom no secrets are hidden, when Martha requested that He act as a judge and bid Mary to rise and help her serve Him, answered for her, because He saw that Mary was fervently occupied in spirit with the love of His Godhead. He did so with great courtesy and as it was reasonable and appropriate for Him to do, because she would not leave her love for Him in order to answer for herself. How did He answer? Certainly not as the judge to whom Martha appealed but as an advocate who lawfully defended the one who loved Him, saying "Martha, Martha." He named her twice, for He wanted her to hear and heed His words. "You are anxious and worried about many things." For actives must be busy and occupied with many things to provide for their own needs and for their deeds of mercy to their fellow Christians, as charity requires. He said this to Martha because He wanted her to know that her activity was good and profitable for the health of her soul. But so she would not think it was the best work someone might do, He added, "But one thing is necessary." [15]

And what is this one thing? Surely that God be loved and praised for Himself above all other bodily or spiritual activity. He said this so Martha might not think that she could love God and praise Him above all other bodily and spiritual activity and also be busy about the necessities of this life. And to prevent her from thinking she might serve God perfectly by combining physical and spiritual activity (imperfectly she might, but not perfectly), He added that Mary had chosen the better part, which should not be taken from her. For the perfect movement of love that begins here on earth is the same as that which lasts forever in the blessedness of heaven. For it is all one.

Entering the Cloud

- *Do you agree that contemplatives should not worry about the complaints of others and that they should simply place these concerns in God's hands?*

- *Do you agree that they should occupy themselves solely with gazing upon the Godhead and resting in its presence?*

- *Do you agree that Mary has indeed chosen the best part and that the contemplative way she embraces represents a purer form of love than that expressed by her sister, Martha?*

- *Do you agree with the author's interpretation of Jesus' response to Martha? Do you agree that his words are not intended as a reprimand but as a loving affirmation of the goodness (and limitations) of the active way?*

- *Do you agree that the contemplative way represents a purer and more complete way of loving God?*

- *Do you disagree with or feel challenged by anything the author says about the nature of active and contemplative ways?*

Chapter Twenty-one

The correct understanding of the Gospel verse:
"Mary has chosen the best part."

Background

In this chapter, the author explains what it means for us "to choose the best part," a verse he would have read in the Latin Vulgate, the only version of Scripture available to him at the time. The Latin "Maria optimam partem elegit" translates literally into English: "Mary has chosen the best part." The word "best," he tells us, refers to more than a simple twofold comparison between the contemplative and active ways as represented in lives of Mary and Martha. As a superlative, "best" requires both a positive and a comparative, that is to say, something "good" and also something "better." He extends this threefold comparison of "good," "better," and "best" to the various ways in which the active and contemplative lives interact. While he is quick to point out that all of these forms of Christian discipleship are good and holy, he insists that they relate to one another in the manner of "good," "better," and "best." The first stage of the active life focuses solely on the corporal acts of mercy and is "good." The second stage of the active (also the first stage of the contemplative) emphasizes good works as well as meditative prayer and is "better." The second stage of the contemplative life turns away from active works entirely to look into the cloud of unknowing and is "best." The author also tells us that the active and the mixed life of action and contemplation will end with the present life because there will be no one in need in the afterlife. The purely contemplative life, by way of contrast, gives us a foretaste of the beatific vision and will last forever.

TEXT

WHAT does this mean: "Mary has chosen the best part?" Whenever we say something is "best," we imply that something "good" and "better" comes before it. What is "best" is thus third in number. But what are these three good things, of which Mary chose the "best?" They are not three lives, for Holy Church recognizes only two: the active and contemplative, seen in this Gospel story in these two sisters, Martha (the active) and Mary (the contemplative). Without following one of these lives, no one can be saved. When there are only two, however, no one can choose the "best."

But although there are only two lives, these two have three parts, each one better than the other. These three parts have been set out in their proper order earlier in this book. The first part, as we said before, consists of good and honest physical works of mercy and of charity. This is the first degree of active life. The second part lies in good spiritual meditations on our own wretchedness, the Passion of Christ, and of the joys of heaven. While the first part is good, this part is better, for it is the second degree of active life and the first of contemplative life. In this part, the contemplative and active lives are coupled together in spiritual kinship and made sisters like Martha and Mary. An active may come to this height of contemplation, but no higher, except rarely and by a special grace. A contemplative may descend this low to the active life, but no lower, except on rare occasions and when there is great need.

The third part of these two lives hangs in this dark cloud of unknowing and has many secret acts of love pressed to God. The first part is good, the second is better, but the third is best of all. This is the "best part" of Mary. And therefore it is plain why our Lord did not say that Mary has chosen the best "life," for there are only two lives, and of two no one can choose the best. Of these two lives, however, He said that Mary had chosen the best part, which would never be taken from her. Although they are good and holy, the first and second parts end with this life. In the life to come there will be no need for the works of mercy, or to weep for our wretchedness, or for the Passion of Christ. For then no one will hunger or thirst, or die of cold, or be sick, or homeless, or in prison, or even in need of burial—for then no one shall die. Let him choose the third part that Mary chose, who has been called by God's grace to do so. Let him strive for it with all his heart; it will never be taken away. Although it begins here, it will last forever.

Therefore, let the voice of our Lord cry to actives, as if He were speaking to them on our behalf as He once did for Mary to Martha, "Martha, Martha!"—"Actives, actives! Be as busy as you can in the first two parts, first in one, then in the other, and vigorously in both if you truly desire it and are so disposed. But do not meddle with contemplatives. You do not know what troubles them. Let them sit in their resting and in their play with the third and best part chosen by Mary."

Entering the Cloud

- *Do you agree with the author's interpretation of what it means to chose "the best part?"*
- *Do you agree that the active, mixed, and purely contemplative parts are "good," "better," and "best?" Must they be compared with each other in this way?*
- *Do you agree that the active life will cease in the afterlife because no one will be in need as they are here on earth?*
- *Do you agree that life in the afterlife involves nothing but contemplating the Godhead?*
- *Can you think of another way of speaking about the active, mixed, and contemplative parts?*
- *Where would you place yourself along this spectrum of "good," "better," and "best?"*

Chapter Twenty-two

The wonderful love Christ had for all sinners who are truly converted and called to the grace of contemplation.

Background

In this chapter, the author explores the mutual and reciprocal love of Jesus and Mary. As with most medieval writers, he identifies Mary, the sister of Martha, with Mary Magdalene and the woman caught in adultery. Recent historical exegesis, by way of contrast, tends to see them as three distinct historical figures. The author's interpretation of Mary is much more figurative than historical. He sees in her a symbol or type of all habitual sinners who have converted to the Lord and embarked on the way of pure contemplation. Mary's love for him is great because she is aware of the depth of God's love and mercy for her. She loves much, because she has been forgiven much. She has such a deep love for Jesus that nothing will comfort her but the Lord himself. Not even the good news of the angels that he has risen from the dead and gone on ahead to Galilee will ease her painful longing. Jesus, in turn, loves Mary with an even deeper and purer love. This love is not of the fleshy, carnal type, but one completely rooted in the mystery of the Godhead. It springs from the depth of his divine mercy and staunchly defends all who, like Mary, are criticized for choosing the best part.

Text

SWEET was the love between our Lord and Mary. Much love had she for Him. Much more had He for her. For whoever would see all that passed between Him and her, not as a casual observer might tell it, but as the story of the Gospel gives witness—which in no way may be false—He would find that her love for Him was so deep and heartfelt that nothing other than Him would comfort her or keep her heart from Him. This is the same Mary who would not be comforted by angels when she sought Him at the sepulcher. [16] When they spoke to her, so graciously saying, "Weep not, Mary, because our Lord whom you seek is risen, and you will have Him and see that He is with His disciples in Galilee, alive in all His beauty," as He said, she would not stop weeping before them. And why? Because she was seeking the King of Angels and would not stop for mere angels.

What more? Surely whoever examines the Gospel story with care will find many wonderful examples of her perfect love written for our benefit, and so closely in accord with this book's teaching that they appear to have been written precisely with that in mind. And so they were, regardless of what anyone says. And anyone disposed to see in the Gospel the special and wonderful love that our Lord had for Mary, the symbol of all habitual sinners who are truly converted and called to the grace of contemplation, he will find that our Lord will not allow any man or woman—yes, not even her own sister—to speak a word against her but will defend her Himself. Moreover, He rebuked Simon the leper in his own home because he was critical of her in thought. [17] This is a great, indeed, overwhelming love.

Entering the Cloud

- *Is a figurative approach to the Gospels still valid today? Can it be used in conjunction with the approach of historical exegesis?*

- *Do you agree with the author's interpretation of Mary?*

- *Do you agree with his depiction of the mutual and reciprocal love of Jesus and Mary?*

- *Do you agree that Mary can be seen as a figure or type of all habitual sinners who have converted to the Lord and set out upon the contemplative way?*

- *Do you agree that the greatest sinners often become the greatest contemplatives?*

- *How deeply are you aware of your own sinfulness?*

- *How deeply are you attracted to the contemplative way?*

Chapter Twenty-three

*How God will spiritually answer and provide for those who,
because of their love for Him, have no desire to answer
or provide for themselves.*

Background

In this chapter, the author reminds us of God's desire to care for
both our physical and spiritual needs. If we are truly converted,
we will not focus on our own sinfulness but rely instead on God's
grandeur and worthiness both in this world and in the world to
come. If we have truly given ourselves over to a life of pure contemplation, we must trust God to convert the hearts of those who
criticize us so that they will soon be ashamed of themselves. Nor
must we allow the lack of material goods to keep us from the path
of pure contemplation. Those of us who have given ourselves over
to this life must trust in the Lord for all our needs. We must believe
that he will give us either an abundance of what we need or the
necessary bodily and spiritual strength to do without.

If we fail to trust in God for our simplest, most basic needs, then
we have not yet been fully converted or, worse still, have possibly
allowed the evil one to gain access to our hearts and sow there
the seeds of doubt. One who possesses God possesses all things.
True humility comes not from focusing on our sinful past but
by allowing God's glory to reign in our hearts. Like Mary, those
called to a life of pure contemplation become humble by casting
our sinful past into the cloud of forgetting and allowing the Lord
to gain sole possession of their hearts.

TEXT

WITHOUT a doubt, if we seriously conform our love and way of life, as best we can, and by grace and spiritual counsel, to Mary's love and way of life, He will answer us spiritually in the same way each day in the hearts of all those who criticize us. I do not say that people will never again speak ill of us as we struggle in life, as they did Mary. But I say that, if we give no heed to what they say or think or cease our inner spiritual work because of their words and thoughts, as she did, then our Lord will answer them in their hearts (if they be sincere) so that within a few days they will be ashamed of their words and thoughts.

As He will answer for us in this way, so will He move others in their hearts to give us the necessities of life: food, clothing, and the like, if He sees that we will not leave the work of loving Him to attend to these matters. I say this to refute the error that says it is wrong to serve God in the contemplative life unless adequate provisions have been secured beforehand. For they say that God sends the cow, but not by the horn. And truly they speak mistakenly of God, as they well know. For you can be sure that if you have truly left the world for God, you will, independently of your own efforts, receive from God one of two things: either an abundant supply of your necessities or the physical strength and spiritual patience to do without. So what does it matter what we have? It is all the same to the true contemplative. Whoever doubts this has either the devil in his breast, depriving him of faith, or is not so truly converted to God as he should be, however shrewd he may be and whatever devout and holy reasons he may give.

Therefore, you who set out to be a contemplative as Mary was, choose instead to be humbled by the greatness and the majesty of God's perfection rather than by your own wretchedness and imperfection. That is to say, look more to God's worthiness than to your own worthlessness. The perfectly humble lack nothing physical or spiritual. For they have God, who possesses all things, and whoever has Him, as this book relates, needs nothing else in this life.

Entering the Cloud

- *Do you agree that to be completely converted, we must rely on God for all our needs?*

- *Has the author adequately identified these needs as being primarily physical and spiritual?*

- *What other needs should we seek from God? The emotional? The intellectual? The social?*

- *Are you in touch with all of your needs? Are you able to identify them? Are you able to bring them to God? Do you believe they will be met despite your sinful past?*

- *Do you focus too much on your past sins? Do such thoughts interfere with your love of God?*

- *What does it mean to be perfectly humble?*

Chapter Twenty-four

*The essence of charity and how it is truly and perfectly
contained in the contemplative work described in this book.*

Background

In this chapter, the author shifts his focus from humility to charity. He tells us that, as with humility, we acquire the virtues by allowing the blind impulse of love within us to beat against the cloud of unknowing. This insight is especially true for the virtue of charity, which he describes as nothing but loving God above all things. True charity, he tells us, means seeking nothing but God for his own sake and asking for nothing in return. We do so by striving to do God's will and not being concerned with whatever joy or pain might be involved. When we love God above all things, he goes on to say, our love for others is also perfected. Loving God for his own sake, which is the first branch of charity, purifies our love for our neighbor, which is the second. He tells us that we know our love for others has been purified when we treat everyone the same, without any special regard for relatives and friends. We look upon all people, even our enemies and those who cause us pain, as God's children and treat them all as we would our closest friends.

TEXT

AS humility is truly and perfectly summed up in this little blind love of God, when it is beat upon this dark cloud of unknowing with all other things put down and forgotten, so are all other virtues, especially charity.

For charity is nothing more than loving God for Himself above all created things and loving others in God as we love ourselves. It is right that in this work of contemplation God is loved in Himself and above all creatures. As we have said before, the substance of this work is nothing more than a naked intent directed to God Himself.

I call it a naked intent because in this work of contemplation a perfect apprentice asks not to be released from pain or rewarded with generosity or to receive anything else but God Himself. So much so that he does not care whether he is in pain or in bliss but only that he follows the will of the one he loves. And so, in this work of contemplation, God is perfectly loved for Himself and above all created things. For in this work, a contemplative may not allow the thought of even the holiest thing to divide his attention.

In doing so, the contemplative fulfills the second, lower branch of charity, concerning the love of our fellow Christians. For the true contemplative has no special esteem for anyone—whether kin or stranger, friend or foe—since he thinks of everyone as his kin and no one as a stranger. He considers everyone his friend and no one his foe, so much so that he considers all those who hurt him and do him injury in this life as his true and special friends, and he desires for them as much good as he does for his closest friend.

Entering the Cloud

- *Do you agree that charity means loving God above all things and for his own sake?*
- *Do you believe it is possible for frail human beings to love God in this way? Can we do it alone? Do we need God's help?*
- *Do you believe that loving God for his own sake purifies our love for others?*
- *Do you agree that love for God must precede our love for others?*
- *How do the two branches of charity relate?*
- *Is love for God more important than love for neighbor? Is it less important? Is it of equal value?*
- *Can you think of an instance in your life where your love for another person was a pure expression of divine love and not in some way influenced by other attachments?*

Chapter Twentyfive

During this work of contemplation, the perfect soul
has no special regard for anyone in this life.

Background

In this chapter, the author tells us that those who enter the cloud of unknowing seek to foster no special human relationships or creaturely affections. While they are in the cloud, they are focused entirely on God and nothing else. Whenever they find themselves in human company, they treat all people the same way. Friend and foe, relative and stranger are all deemed worthy of the same loving attention. They look upon others from a divine rather than human perspective and relate to them accordingly. They can do so, the author tells us, because when entering the company of others, they never fully leave the heights of pure contemplation but carry an awareness of the divine presence with them wherever they go. Nor do they have the leisure to develop such relationships, since their primary focus is to beat against the cloud of unknowing with the impulse of divine love and cast everything else into the cloud of forgetting.

That is not to say that, like the Lord himself, they do not feel drawn at times to some people more than others. It simply means that those who have chosen the path of pure contemplation will love others as God loves them and to the same degree. To support this claim, the author employs the Pauline metaphor of the Church as the body of Christ. By virtue of Adam's sin, we are all brothers and sisters in desperate need of the redemption wrought by Christ's paschal mystery. Those who wish to be true disciples of Christ must understand that they are members of Christ's body and that their experience of pure contemplation in the cloud of unknowing is not meant for them alone. In the midst of this exercise, they must be willing to lift their spirits up for the salvation of all humanity, just as Christ lifted up his body on the cross.

TEXT

I SAY he shall not have a special regard for anyone in this life, whether he be friend or foe, kin or stranger, since that cannot be in perfect contemplation when, as is fitting, all things under God are fully forgotten. But I say he will become so virtuous and charitable through this work, that afterward, when he descends from the heights to converse or pray for his fellow Christians, he will be as easily directed toward his foe as to his friend, toward a stranger as to his kin. Yes, and sometimes even more to his foes than to his friends!

Nevertheless, in this work of contemplation he has no leisure to look after his friend or his foe, his kin or his stranger. I say this not because he will not sometimes (even often) feel more affection toward one, two, or three than to all others. That is only right and, in many cases, required by charity. Christ felt deep affection for John, Mary, and Peter before many others. But I say that in this work of contemplation the soul completely immersed in God will have equal affection for everyone. All are loved plainly and simply for God's sake as well as his own.

For as all men are lost in Adam and reveal by their works their desire for salvation and are saved by virtue of Christ's passion (and nothing else) in the same manner, a soul perfectly disposed to contemplation and one with God gives witness by doing all it can to make everyone as perfect as itself. For when a limb of our body feels pain, all the other limbs suffer with it, and when the limb is sound, the others rejoice with it. So it is spiritually with all the members of Holy Church. For Christ is our head and, if we abide in charity, we are the limbs. Whoever wishes to be a perfect disciple of our Lord must strain the muscles of his spirit in this spiritual work to save all his brothers and sisters, just as our Lord did with His body on the Cross. He does this not only for his closest friends and relations but for all humanity, without any more special regard to one than to another. For all who forsake sin and ask for mercy will be saved by Christ's passion. What we say of humility and charity is valid for all other virtues. As stated earlier, they are all involved in this little pressing action of love.

Entering the Cloud

- Do you have any close friendships that you cherish more than others?

- Do you possess anything to which you are inordinately attached?

- Do you agree that following the way of pure contemplation involves casting all human relationships and affection for creaturely objects into the cloud of forgetting?

- Is it possible to be a true disciple of Christ without entering the cloud of unknowing?

- Why must the pure contemplative be willing to let go of all human friendships and creaturely attachments? Why must he or she offer up the experience in the darkness of the cloud for the salvation of all humanity?

- Are you capable of doing what the author asks? Would you like to be? Are you willing to bring it to prayer and ask for guidance?

Chapter Twenty-Six

Without special grace or habitual cooperation with ordinary grace, this work of contemplation is extremely difficult; the distinction between the soul helped by grace and the work of God alone.

Background

In this chapter, the author details the great difficulty those called to pure contemplation have in entering into and ultimately penetrating the cloud of unknowing. We can hope to persevere in this arduous task only with the help of a special grace of God or by our continual cooperation with the ordinary graces received in everyday life. He goes on to say that the activity of the soul inspired by grace involves casting all created things into the cloud of forgetting. The soul's actual penetration of the cloud of unknowing, by way of contrast, comes from the direct activity of the Godhead. It alone can ignite the impulse of divine love in a person's heart that will pierce the cloud's darkness and lead to a direct experience of the beyond.

Passing through the cloud of unknowing is thus both a work of human cooperation with God's grace and the direct action of God himself. We cooperate with God's grace by casting all creaturely attachments into the cloud of forgetting. The soul enters into and ultimately penetrates the surrounding darkness, however, only as a result of the direct activity of God himself. The author encourages us to press ahead by continuing to beat against the cloud of unknowing with the impulse of divine love. In time, God will send us a beam of spiritual light that will pierce the surrounding darkness, dissipate it, and help us to see what lies beyond. Indeed, God promises to reveal his deepest secrets to us if we but agree to set out on this long and toilsome journey—and allow God to do his work in us. Man was once the master of all created things. After the Fall, however, he became a slave to all earthly passions and desires. Our journey from the cloud of forgetfulness into the cloud of unknowing is another way of speaking about humanity's restoration to its rightful place in the order of creation.

TEXT

SO work hard at it! Beat upon this high cloud of unknowing—and rest afterward! It is a difficult work for whoever undertakes it. Yes, indeed! It is a very hard work, unless one receives a special grace from God or has spent a long time at it.

How is it difficult? Surely not in the devout movement of love in the will, produced not by oneself but by the hand of Almighty God, who is ever ready to work in each soul disposed to Him and does all it can to prepare itself for this work.

So where is the hard work? No doubt it is in pressing down the memory of all God's creatures and, as mentioned before, in holding them under the cloud of forgetting. Here lies the hard work, and it is our work, aided by grace. And the other, as mentioned above—that is, the stirring of love—is the work of God alone. So do your work and I promise you He shall not fail in his.

Do your work then—and with dispatch! Let me see how you carry yourself. Can you not see that He is standing and waiting for you? Shame on you! Work hard for a little while and you will soon find the immensity and difficulty of this work begin to relent. For it is hard and narrow in the beginning, when you have no devotion. Later, however, when you have devotion, what was hard to bear will become restful and easy. And you will have little or no work to do, for God will sometimes work in you all by Himself. But He will not do so for long and only when He likes and as He likes it. Then you will be happy to let Him have His way with you.

At such times, He will send out a beam of spiritual light, piercing this cloud of unknowing between you and Him and show you some of His secrets, of which we are not allowed or able to speak. Then you will feel your affection inflamed with the fire of His love, far more than I can possibly tell you at this time. I dare not speak with my blabbering, fleshly tongue of that work which falls to God alone. I dare not say anything about it. But of that work which falls to man when he feels himself moved and helped by grace, I will gladly speak, for that is the less risky of the two.

Entering the Cloud

- *Do you agree that entering into and breaking through the cloud of unknowing is a long and arduous task, one that requires special graces from God or, at the very least, habitual cooperation with the ordinary graces received in everyday life?*

- *Do you agree that this journey has the twofold function of casting all creaturely affections into the cloud of forgetting and allowing the impulse of divine love to beat upon and ultimately penetrate the cloud of unknowing?*

- *Does God call everyone to the cloud of unknowing? Does he call everyone to it in this life or perhaps in the life to come?*

- *Has God called you to this special vocation of pure contemplation? If so, have you asked God for the necessary graces? Are you prepared for the long, toilsome journey that lies ahead?*

Chapter Twenty-seven

Who should undertake the gracious work of contemplation?

Background

In this chapter, the author conveys a very important message in a handful of well-chosen words. He tells us that not everyone should attempt to enter and ultimately penetrate the cloud of unknowing, but only those who have forsaken the things of this world for a life of pure contemplation. Since this exercise involves a twofold process of casting all thoughts and creaturely attachments into the cloud of forgetting and then continually knocking on the cloud of unknowing with the impulse of divine love, he implies that those entering the cloud who have not yet completely left behind the things of this world must have a sincere desire to do so. Those in the first stage of contemplation which, like the second stage of the active life, is a mixture of action and contemplation, may enter the cloud, but only if they are intent on ultimately leaving the active life behind and embracing a life of pure contemplation. As we penetrate the cloud of unknowing, the cloud of forgetting is itself gradually forgotten, and the darkness of the cloud itself dissipates through the direct action of the Godhead.

TEXT

FIRST and foremost, I will tell you who should practice this work of contemplation, and when, and how, and what precautions they must take. If you ask me who should take it up, I would say, "All who have freely and completely forsaken the world and given themselves not to active life but to the contemplative. They should take up this work by grace, whoever that they may be, whether or not they have been habitual sinners."

Entering the Cloud

- *What does the author mean by "forsaking the world?" Entering a monastery for a life of pure contemplation? Living a mixed life of action and contemplation, but with a deep desire to one day leave the active life behind?*

- *Why is the world of activity and thought so foreign to the world of the pure contemplative?*

- *In what ways can the author's words be adapted to today's world?*

- *Is it possible for even the pure contemplative to leave behind all thought and action in this world?*

- *How is entering the cloud and performing the exercise proposed by the author a real possibility for you?*

- *Is it possible to adapt his thought to today's world without compromising his teaching?*

Chapter Twentyeight

No one should dare take up this work before being lawfully absolved in conscience of all particular sins.

Background

In this chapter, the author emphasizes the importance of having a clear conscience for those wishing to enter the state of pure contemplation. We cleanse our consciences by going to the sacrament of penance, where we have the opportunity to confess our sins—both mortal and venial—and receive forgiveness by a lawful representative of Christ and his Church. It would be futile for any of us to attempt to undertake this exercise without first having cleansed our souls of sin by these ordinary sacramental means. He goes on to say that, as a result of humanity's fall from grace, this thick cloud of unknowing comes between us and our experience of God. One of the greatest effects of Adam's sin is that we, who once had stewardship and lordship over the things of this world, are now ruled by them. This is evidenced most clearly by the way the desire for creaturely things inserts itself into our thoughts, prevents us from keeping God's law, and interferes with our love for our creator. As a result, what should be beneath us imposes itself from above and comes between us and the God who made us.

TEXT

BUT if you ask me when they should undertake this work of contemplation, I answer: "Not before they have cleansed their conscience of all their past sins in accordance with the common ordinances of Holy Church."

For in this work of contemplation, a soul dries up the root and ground of sin that remains in it, even after confession and regardless of how reverent it is. Therefore, whoever undertakes this work, let him first cleanse his conscience, and afterward, when he has made amends, let him give himself to it boldly but humbly. Let him remember how long he has stayed away from it. This is the work a person should perform throughout his life, even if he has never committed a serious sin. As long as a soul dwells in this mortal flesh, he shall always see and feel this burdensome cloud of unknowing between him and God. Moreover, because of original sin, he will always see and feel that some of God's creatures, or some of their works, are pressing in his mind between him and God. This is part of God's wisdom and justice. That is to say that man, the sovereign lord of all other creatures, who deliberately made himself a slave to his subjects by leaving the command of God his Maker, would afterward keep God's commands by seeing and feeling all the creatures that should be beneath him, proudly insert themselves above him, between him and his God.

Entering the Cloud

- *Why must those who enter the cloud of unknowing do so with a clear conscience? Is it because the moral life is intimately connected to the spiritual life? Is it because the way of perfection presupposes that we have traveled the purgative and illuminative ways? Is it because God, the source of all goodness, will not enter into fellowship with someone who refuses to cleanse his heart?*

- *Why is the sacrament of reconciliation the best way to clear our consciences? Is it because through it Christ himself forgives us our sins and heals us with sanctifying grace? Is it because through the words of absolution, it gives us a concrete sign that we have, in fact, been forgiven?*

- *Do you see the sacrament as a way of cleansing your conscience, reordering your desires, and preparing you for an intimate experience of God?*

- *What other ways are there for cleansing our consciences?*

Chapter Twenty-nine

A man should persevere in this work of contemplation,
endure its pain, and judge no one.

Background

In this chapter, the author highlights the importance of perseverance for those who enter the cloud of unknowing in search of God and a life of pure contemplation. This life is not for the faint-hearted. Those who undertake this exercise of casting all thought into the cloud of forgetting and knocking on the dark, seemingly impermeable cloud of unknowing with the impulse of divine love must be willing to endure the pain that comes with it. Everyone, saints and sinners alike, will find this exercise difficult and painstaking. Although those who were habitual sinners in the past will generally find this exercise more difficult than those who have led more innocent and sheltered lives, it is not uncommon for those who have sunk into the depths of corruption to rise more quickly to the heights of contemplation than others. The author calls this a "miracle of our Lord's mercy" and emphasizes the gratuitousness of God's grace and his desire to show the world the extent of his compassion, love, and forgiveness. For this reason, we should not be quick to judge others but leave them instead to the Lord's justice. We should condemn the sin, not the sinner. The author reminds us that those who seem to us the greatest of sinners may be exalted at the end of time, while those who appear to have led saintly lives may be exposed as hypocrites before the judgment seat of the Lord.

TEXT

THEREFORE, whoever desires to regain the cleanness he lost through sin and to attain that well-being bereft of grief, he must patiently keep at this work and suffer its pain, whoever he is, whether he has been a habitual sinner or not.

Everyone finds this work very difficult: both sinners and innocents who never gravely sinned. But those who have been sinners have much more work to do than those who have not, and understandably so. Still, it often happens that some who have been horrible and habitual sinners come to the perfection of contemplation sooner than those who have not. This is a miracle of our Lord's mercy, who to the world's wonderment has given them His special grace. I truly hope that the day of judgment will be fair and lovely, when God and all His gifts will be clearly seen. On that day, some now despised and considered little or nothing because they are common sinners (and perhaps some who are horrible sinners) will sit with saints in His presence. And some who now seem so holy and almost worshiped by men as angels, and perhaps some who have never sinned mortally, will sit most sorrowfully in the caves of hell.

By this you will see that people should not be judged by another in this life for the good or evil they do. Actions may be judged good or evil, but not the person.

Entering the Cloud

- *Why is perseverance so important for the Christian life? Why is it especially important for those who follow the contemplative way?*

- *Do you consider yourself someone capable of enduring intense hardship?*

- *Is such courage and endurance in the midst of adversity a natural endowment, something that can be developed over time, or a gift from God? What about judging others?*

- *Do you agree that we should judge a person's actions as good or evil, but not the person?*

- *Do you find it difficult to refrain from judging others? Have you ever felt unfairly judged by another?*

- *What does withholding judgment of others have to do with perseverance? What does it have to do with the contemplative way? What does it have to do with the way of Christian discipleship?*

Chapter Thirty

Who should judge the deeds of others?

Background

In this chapter, the author makes his thoughts on judging the actions of others a bit more precise. While no one should take it upon his or her own authority to judge another person's faults, he recognizes that those entrusted by Christ with the pastoral care of souls have a role to play in judging the behavior of the people they serve. He also recognizes that certain individuals (a spiritual director, for example) may be led interiorly by the Holy Spirit to confront a person in a similar way. For the most part, however, we should not take it upon ourselves to judge another person's flaws unless we are convinced that we have been given the authority to do so. He tells us that we should be more concerned with judging our own misdeeds and foibles, a matter that lies strictly between us and God, with the possible help of a spiritual director.

TEXT

WHO should judge men's deeds? Surely those who have power over and care for their souls and who have been given official authority by the statute and the ordinance of Holy Church, or else spiritually and in confidence through movement of the Holy Spirit in perfect charity. We must be careful not to blame and condemn the faults of others, unless we feel truly moved to do so by the Holy Spirit. Otherwise, we might be entirely wrong. Beware, therefore. Judge yourself if you wish—you and your God, or your spiritual father—and leave others alone.

Entering the Cloud

- *Do you agree that we should not concern ourselves with the faults of others unless we have been granted lawful ecclesiastical authority or have received a clear internal prompting of the Holy Spirit?*

- *Do you agree that, for the most part, we should be concerned with our own faults and not those of others?*

- *Is the author overemphasizing institutional authority in this chapter? Is he overemphasizing spiritual, charismatic piety?*

- *Where does sincere brotherly correction enter into the author's perspective? Do you agree that such correction has both an institutional (ecclesiastical) and a charismatic (inspirational and prophetic) dimension to it?*

- *Have you ever been corrected by someone for a misdeed or character flaw? Was it done appropriately or from false motivations?*

- *How do we know when to say something to a brother or a sister who has behaved badly?*

Chapter Thirtyone

How to act when beginning this work against all sinful thoughts and impulses.

Background

In this chapter, the author tells us what to do once we have repented of and done penance for our sins according to the norms and regulations of the Church. He says we must begin by eagerly adopting the task before us and casting any sins that subsequently enter our awareness into the cloud of forgetting. We do so by countering this tendency toward sin with a deeply passionate impulse of love. In this way, we will be able to trample down fresh temptations, as well as the memories of past sins. If we find this overly burdensome, he says we can learn certain lessons from God to help us put these evil thoughts out of our minds.

TEXT

WHEN you feel you have done all you can to amend yourself to God according to the lawful ordinances of Holy Church, then you can dedicate yourself entirely to this work. If memories of your past life keep coming between you and God, or any new thought or impulse toward sin, you must resolutely step above them with a fervent movement of love and trample them under your feet. Try to cover them with a thick cloud of forgetting, as though they had never been committed in this life by you or anyone else. Put them down as often as they arise in your mind. And if you think the work difficult, use whatever arts, wiles, and spiritual subtleties you can to put them away. It is better to learn these spiritual arts from God than from anyone else.

Entering the Cloud

- *Are you eager and excited about entering the cloud of unknowing and beating against it with the impulse of heartfelt love? Do you look forward to this exercise? Are you passionate about it?*

- *How do you deal with the sins of your past? Have you put them solidly behind you, or do you feel haunted by them, even after you have confessed them and made reparation for them?*

- *How do you deal with fresh temptations? Do you recognize them for what they are and confront them immediately? Have you ever felt overwhelmed by them and found it difficult to put them out of your mind?*

- *Have your ways of dealing with evil thoughts—old or new—worked for you? Are you open to learning new ways of dealing with them?*

Chapter Thirty-two

Two spiritual helps for the beginner in this work of contemplation.

Background

In this chapter, the author gives us two pieces of advice on how to conquer evil thoughts. He admits in the last chapter that the best person to learn these lessons from is God, but he wishes at this point of his discourse to share with us a bit of his own experience. He bids us to try his suggestions out and encourages us to find other practices that might work for us. In saying this, he is implying that there are any number of ways of coping with evil temptations and that we must seek out those practices that work best for us. As far as his own experience goes, he tells us first "to look over the shoulder" of those evil thoughts that enter our awareness and come between us and God. By this he means we should act as though these thoughts are not as severe and troubling as they make themselves out to be and that we should act as though we are really looking for something else. This "something else," of course, is God and the dark cloud surrounding him. He assures us that acting in this way will make these thoughts seem less troubling and burdensome. He describes how this little trick or coping mechanism puts us in touch with our longing for God and our desire to see him. It is a manifestation of charity and helps us remember our true end and our very reason for entering the cloud of unknowing.

The second bit of advice he asks us to try out is to collapse helplessly in the face of these evil thoughts as if we were melting in water. This way of dealing with temptation helps us to recognize our inability to defeat evil by our own power. It puts us in touch with our human frailty and deep need for God at all times. When we face temptation in this way, we recognize the extent of our corrupted natures and come to understand our total impotence before the power of evil. This awareness deepens our humility by giving us a true knowledge of ourselves before God. In the face of these pressing and overpowering thoughts, he tells us that God will intervene on our behalf as a father rescues his child from wild beasts. In doing so, he will lift us from the clutches of evil, comfort us, and dry our spiritual eyes.

Text

STILL, I can teach you something of these spiritual arts. Try them out and see if you can do better. Do all you can to act as if you did not know they were pressing in so strongly between you and God. Try to look, as it were, over their shoulders, seeking something else: your God, who is shrouded in a cloud of unknowing. And if you do this, I believe that within a short while you will find your work much easier. I believe that if this spiritual help is well understood and implemented, it will show itself to be nothing but a deep longing for God, a desire to experience and see Him as one may do so here below. Such a desire is charity, and it always deserves to be made easier.

Here is another spiritual help to try if you wish. Whenever you feel that you are unable to put these thoughts aside, cower down under them like a coward overcome in battle and think that it is useless for you to strive any longer against them. Surrender yourself to God while in the hands of your enemies and feel as though you were overcome forever. Take heed of this suggestion, for I think that, if you try it out, it will dissolve all opposition. I am sure that, if this spiritual help is properly understood, it is nothing else but a true knowledge and experience of yourself as you are: wretched, filthy, and far worse than nothing. Such knowledge and experience is humility. And this humility causes God Himself to descend mightily, avenge you against your enemies, take you up, and dry your spiritual eyes with affection, as a father does his child who is about to perish in the mouths of wild boars or ferocious, growling bears.

118

Entering the Cloud

- *Have you discovered any concrete ways of dealing with evil thoughts and desires? If so, what are they? How did you discover them? How long did it take you to find them? Do they always work? Have you tried certain practices that were not helpful to you? What about the author's suggestions?*

- *Do you think "looking over the shoulder" of evil thoughts and desires will lessen their impact and make them less threatening? Will it help you to recognize them for what they really are? Will it put you in touch with your longing for God? Will simply collapsing before them in total help-lessness deepen your humility by putting you in touch with your complete powerlessness in the face of evil? Will it call up God to intervene on your behalf?*

- *What other possible outcomes could either of these coping mechanisms have?*

Chapter Thirtythree

In this work of contemplation, a soul is cleansed of both particular sins and the pain related to them; there is no perfect rest in this life.

Background

In this chapter, the author decides not to share with us any further ways of dealing with evil thoughts and desires, at least not for the time being. He encourages us instead to test his suggestions on ourselves. He even expresses a hope of learning something from our own experiences about how he might progress in his own spiritual journey. If we find that his suggestions do not work for us and we feel helpless before the evil thoughts that rage about us, he bids us to carry on and put up with the accompanying pain and discomfort as best we can. If we do so humbly and with the right motivations, he assures us that God will enable us to persevere by giving us the grace to acquire the appropriate habits of mind that will purify us of our past sins and their harmful effects. He is not referring here to original sin, the effects of which will always be with us on our earthly sojourn.

Even though these effects may not trouble us as much as those of our own personal sins, he reminds us that fresh temptations continually arise from our weakened state due to the sin of our first parents. These we must put down as prudently and expeditiously as possible so they will not become unwieldy and eventually overwhelm us. He also reminds us that, because of the effects of original sin and our own personal propensity to sin, we will never be completely free from temptation. But he asks us not to get discouraged or become overly afraid of falling. Even though we will never experience complete and total rest in this life, he assures us that by employing the means he has described for dealing with the sins of our past, we will not be overly troubled by the effects of original sin and any other evil impulses to sin that come our way.

TEXT

I WILL NOT show you any other spiritual helps at this time, for, if you receive the grace to try these, I believe you will soon be better able to teach me than I you. For although I am now teaching you, I myself have a long way to go. And so I ask you to help me as well as yourself.

Go on then and work hard and fast at it, I beg you. Suffer humbly the pain you must endure before mastering these arts. For this is your purgatory. And then when your pain has passed and your spiritual skills given by God and by His grace become habitual, then I have no doubt that you will be cleansed not only of sin but also of the pain of sin. I mean the pain of your past personal sins, not the pain of the original sin. For however hard you work, that pain will stay with you until the day of your death. Nevertheless, in comparison to the pain of your personal sins, this pain will not be a major hindrance to you. Still you will have a great deal of work to do. For from this original sin, new and fresh impulses of sin will always spring, and every day you must put them down and be busy cutting away with a sharp double-edged sword of discretion. So you will learn that there is no real security and no true rest in this life.

Nevertheless, you should not draw back or be afraid of failing. For if you are to receive the grace to destroy the pain of your past personal sins in the manner described above—or in your own way if you can do better—you can be sure that the pain of the original sin, or the impulses to sin it produces, will provoke you but little.

Entering the Cloud

- *Do you believe that, despite your difficulty in overcoming evil thoughts and desires, God will help you through your purgatory and eventually give you the grace to overcome them? Is doing so God's work or yours? In what ways could it be both?*

- *Do you believe that, because of the continuing effects of original sin, the impulse to do wrong will never leave you entirely in this life? Will it leave you entirely in the life to come?*

- *Are you bothered by the impact of original sin and its effects on your life? Are you bothered by the memory of your past sins and their evil effects? Are you bothered by the inability to experience complete rest in this life?*

- *How would you instruct a beginner in the contemplative way in dealing with the onslaught of evil thoughts and desires?*

Chapter Thirty-four

God gives this grace freely without any prior cause;
it does not come through any particular means.

Background

In this chapter, the author emphasizes the total gratuitousness of
God's grace and says that it alone is what enables us to penetrate the
cloud of unknowing. He reminds us that we are totally incapable
of accomplishing this task by ourselves. It is a work of God and no
one else. He goes on to tell us that this grace is not something we
can earn or that we have a right to in any way. God sends this grace
to whomever he pleases—habitual sinners as well as the innocent.
He even suggests that God may choose to bless habitual sinners in
this way more often than those who have caused him little grief.
God dispenses his graces as he pleases, for the Spirit blows where
it wills. Whoever they are—be they saints or sinners—the recipi-
ents of this special grace all have the capacity to receive it and be
elevated to this heightened sphere of consciousness. God chooses
to withhold this grace as he pleases, since it cannot be earned or
merited by anything we do. He withdraws it, however, from anyone who has received it and yet has relapsed and fallen into sin, a
perennial possibility for anyone living in this fallen world. For this
reason, he warns those whom God has blessed with this special
grace to watch out for sin, especially that of pride. We can easily
fall into the error of thinking we are without sin and perhaps even
incapable of sinning. Such an attitude makes us arrogant before
God and is a far cry from the humility of a true disciple of Christ.

The author goes on to say that God's grace bestows upon the
recipient both the capacity for penetrating the cloud of unknowing and the experience itself. The two are intimately linked and
cannot be separated. God gives us both the desire for it and the
capacity to experience it. We should not worry if we do not understand how this all takes place in the deepest recesses of our souls.

The author tells us simply to trust in God and allow his grace to do its work in us. Nor must we get in its way. All we need to do is allow it to happen. We are to allow ourselves to be shaped, as a carpenter works his wood and the homeowner manages his house. We are to embrace our blindness and cast off all desire for knowing. We must recognize that this experience comes not from any intermediary—be it angel or demon (whom we therefore need not fear)—but from God alone. He alone moves our wills and plants the desire for it in our hearts. He alone draws us through the cloud of unknowing and unto himself.

Text

AND if you ask me how to begin this work, I beg Almighty God to teach you Himself through His grace and courtesy. For it is good for you to know that I cannot teach you. That should come as no surprise. For it is the work of God alone, wrought in whatever soul He chooses, regardless of the merits of that particular soul. For without God's help, no saint or angel can even think of desiring it. Moreover, I think our Lord is ready to perform this work as readily and as often, indeed even more so, in those who have been habitual sinners than in those who in comparison never grieved Him very much. And He will do this to be seen as all-merciful and almighty, and to be seen to work as He wishes, where He wishes, and when He wishes.

Yet He does not give this grace or begin this work in any soul unwilling to receive it. No soul, with or without sin, can have this grace without God's help. It is not given on account of one's innocence or withheld on account of one's sin. Notice that I say "withheld" and not "withdrawn." Beware of the error here, I beg you, for the nearer we touch the truth, the more we must guard against error. I think my meaning is clear, but if you cannot understand it now, lay it aside until God comes and teaches you. If you do so, you will not be hurt.

Beware of pride, for it blasphemes God and His gifts and encourages sinners. If you were truly humble, you would feel the same about the contemplative life as I do: that God gives it freely, regardless of merits. The state of contemplation is such that its presence enables a soul to practice it and be aware of it. It is impossible to have this ability without it. The capacity for contemplation is the same as contemplation itself, so that whoever feels he can contemplate is able to do so. No one else can. Without this prior working of God, a soul is, as it were, dead and unable to covet or desire it. Since you will it and desire it, you obviously already have it, and no more or less. Yet is it not your will or desire that moves you, but something you are completely ignorant of, stirring you to will and desire you know not what? I beg you not to worry if you never know more than this, but go on ever more and more so that you will continue to advance.

To be brief, let this thing deal with you and lead you wherever it wishes. Let it be active, and you be passive. Watch it, but let it alone. Do not meddle with it, as though you would help it, for fear that you should spoil it all. Be the tree and let it be the carpenter; be the house and let it be the owner who dwells there. Be blind for now and shear away the longing to know, for knowing will be more of a hindrance than a help to you. It suffices that you feel yourself moved lovingly by you know not what, and that in this stirring you have no special thought of anything other than God, and that your desire is simply directed to God.

If it is like this with you, then you can be sure that only God Himself moves your will and desire directly without any intervening means on His part or on yours. Do not be afraid then, for the devil cannot come this close. He can only stir a man's will on occasion and from afar, however subtle he may be. Without sufficient means, not even a good angel can touch your will directly. In short, only God can. You can understand by what I have written (but much better by experience) that men come to contemplation directly, without any intervening means. All good means rely on this work of contemplation, but it relies on no such means—nor can they bring one to it.

Entering the Cloud

- *Do you agree that penetrating the cloud of unknowing is entirely a work of God and no one else? Where does human effort fit in?*

- *Is the author endorsing a total passivity before God or simply emphasizing God's sovereignty in all things?*

- *Is he perhaps suggesting that even the difficult spiritual exercise of casting all thought into the cloud of forgetting and beating against the cloud of unknowing with the impulse of divine love has its origins in God himself?*

- *Do you agree that this grace comes to us directly from God without any intermediary means? If so, how does this spirituality explain the sacramental nature of the Church and the workings of the sacraments?*

- *Is he implying that because they mediate God's grace to us, the sacraments ultimately cannot lead us to the direct experience of God himself?*

- *Is he denying the efficacy of the Church's sacramental system or simply presupposing it and pointing to something beyond it?*

- *Does it seem fair that God gives this special grace of penetrating the cloud of unknowing to whomever he pleases?*

- *Does God favor some more than others? Does he bless some with deeper revelations and experiences of divine love than others? Are some souls given a greater capacity for expressing divine love than others?*

Chapter Thirtyfive

A beginning contemplative should be occupied with reading,
meditating, and praying.

Background

In this chapter, the author looks at three important spiritual practices for those just entering the contemplative stage of their spiritual journey: the lesson, the meditation, and the petition. He refers to them more simply as reading, reflection, and prayer. These exercises are extremely important for those just entering the contemplative stage and should be fostered from the very outset of their spiritual journey. For this reason, he addresses his words mainly to those at the earlier stages of the spiritual life: the beginner and the proficient. The author presupposes here knowledge of the three ways of the spiritual life that in his day were already deeply rooted in the Christian tradition, dating back to the patristic era and solidified in the medieval monastic and scholastic writings.

These stages—the purgative (for beginners), the illuminative (for the proficient), and the unitive (for the perfect)—are best distinguished by their particular focus: the purgative, with the cleansing and purification of sin; the illuminative, with the development of the moral life growth in the virtues; and the unitive, with mystical union with God and life in the Spirit. Rather than thinking of these stages in strictly linear terms with one stage being left behind for the next, it would be better to think of them as a rising spiral with each stage (and the lessons learned from it) revisited from time to time at appropriate moments of a person's spiritual journey. The author suspects that many (if not most) of his readers will be in these early stages of prayer and so wants to make sure they understand the importance of these basic practices for their entire spiritual journey. If they do not, they will never reach their destination. Those in the unitive stage, moreover, will not stay there for long if they fail to incorporate these foundational practices into their daily spiritual regimen. He goes on to make a number of points about these three important practices. In the first place, they are so closely related that helpful spiritual reflection cannot exist without prior reading. Authentic prayer, in turn, presupposes both meditation and spiritual reading. In a time of widespread illiteracy, the author points out an important connection between listening and reading. When the faithful listen to their priests they are, in a sense, reading the books they share with them through their preaching. He tells us, moreover, that reason is the spiritual eye of the soul and conscience, its spiritual face. Reading or listening to God's Word is like looking into a mirror to see the state of one's spiritual health. Just as we cannot see the dirt on our face without looking into a mirror, so too we are incapable of sensing the stains of sin on our consciousness, unless we look into the mirror of God's Word.

Similarly, if we must go to a well and wash our eyes out with water because they are completely covered with mud, so too habitual sinners blinded by sin must go to the well of the Church and wash themselves in the water of sacramental confession. At this point, he draws a further distinction between the sins we actually commit and the tendency to sin, telling us that we must bring our sins to confession, but that we can treat the tendency to sin through prayer and reliance on God's mercy. Throughout this chapter, the author emphasizes the authority of the Church and its power to forgive sins and encourages us to make full use of the grace of the sacrament and all its elements: contrition, confession, absolution, and satisfaction. He also insists that beginners and the proficient need spiritual reading or listening to arrive at authentic prayer.

TEXT

STILL, there are helps which the apprentice contemplative can use, namely, Lesson, Meditation, and Orison, or as they are better known, Reading, Reflecting, and Praying. These are treated elsewhere by another writer and in a way much better than I can deal with them, and I do need to treat them here. But I can tell you this: These three are so closely related for beginners and proficients—but not for the perfect (in their earthly sojourn)—that reflection may not come unless reading or hearing come first. Reading and hearing are all the same. Clerics read books and the common folk "read" clerics when they hear them preach the word of God. Moreover, beginners and proficients cannot pray without thinking first.

Here is the proof. God's word, written or spoken, is like a mirror. Spiritually, the "eye" of your soul is your reason, while your conscience is your spiritual face. Just as you cannot see a dirty spot on your face without the help of a mirror or without someone telling you, so spiritually it is impossible for a soul blinded by habitual sin to see the dirty spot on his conscience without reading or hearing God's word.

It follows that if a man sees where the dirty spot is on his face, either in a mirror—be it physical or spiritual—or because someone has told him, then, and not until then, he runs to the well to wash himself. If this spot is a personal sin, then the "well" is Holy Church and the "water," confession, and all that goes with it. If it is a deeply rooted sin and given to sinful impulses, then the "well" is our all-merciful God and the "water," prayer, and all that goes with it. So you can see that beginners and proficients cannot meditate without first reading or hearing, or pray without meditating beforehand.

Entering the Cloud

- *Why are reading, meditation, and prayer so important for the spiritual journey?*
- *Why is reading necessary for proper reflection on the truths of the faith and reflection or meditation a prerequisite for prayer?*
- *Do you consider yourself a beginner or proficient at these exercises?*
- *If pure contemplation is a pure gift of God, in what ways are these exercises also gifts? Can someone be given the gift of pure contemplation without them?*
- *Do you understand the distinctions between the purgative, illuminative, and contemplative ways? Why are they important background for the insights the author shares in this chapter?*

- *Do you understand the author's distinction between sin and the impulse to sin? Do you agree with him that the proper place for dealing with sin is sacramental confession, while the tendency to sin can be dealt with through prayer and turning to God's mercy?*
- *Do you like the metaphor of the mirror that he applies to God's Word?*
- *Do you like his metaphor of the Church as a well and sacramental confession as the cleansing water that can be drawn from it?*
- *What other images or metaphors might be helpful in conveying the same ideas?*

Chapter Thirty-Six

The meditations of those dedicated to the work
of contemplation described in this book.

Background

In this chapter, the author focuses on the prayer of the perfect, that is, of those habitually immersed in the practice of pure contemplation. While they have a deep need and respect for reading, meditation, and traditional prayer, and continue to look to them and fall back on them as important foundations for their spiritual journey, they believe the Lord is calling them to leave these things behind at times and to focus their hearts entirely on what cannot be expressed in either thoughts or words. Trusting in these inspirations from the Lord, they leave these good practices behind to concentrate everything in their minds and hearts on the cloud of unknowing and casting everything else into the cloud of forgetting. At such times, their prayer becomes much simpler and they often use a single word such as "sin" or "God" to sum up their recognition of their deep sinfulness and their deep desire for union with the divine.

These single words are also seen as a way of focusing their minds away from all other thoughts and to help them avoid the deliberation and analysis common to meditation and the reflection found in discursive prayer. The primary purpose of these simple prayers, however, is to focus their minds and hearts on what lies beyond the realm of thought and conceptual analysis. As pure contemplatives, they understand that God has revealed himself through his Word, yet is also somehow deeper than his Word. They seek to allow God's grace to draw them into that realm where the ground of the divinity exists in itself as the source of all existence. They seek union with the source of all that is real and have come to understand in their hearts that this ineffable source wishes the same for them. Whenever they find themselves praying in this simple, seemingly irrational way, others will find no observable difference in their outward behavior or countenance. While they may at times experience a kind of spiritual inebriation which makes them feel as though they were somehow outside of themselves, their primary experience of penetrating the cloud and resting in what lies beyond will be one of internal peace and rest with little perceptible change in their physical coordination or bodily movements.

TEXT

BUT it is not so with those who continually practice the work of contemplation described in this book. For them, meditation consists in the sudden recognition and blind experience of their own wretchedness or of God's goodness without any prior help from reading or hearing and with no special meditation on anything whatever. This sudden recognition and blind experience is better learned from God than from man. It does not matter to me if in your life you had no other thoughts of your own wretchedness or of God's goodness—that is, if you feel so moved by grace and spiritual counsel—other than what comes from the word "sin" and from the word "God," or a similar word of your own choosing. Do not try to analyze or explain these words with your own curious mind, as if, by considering their parts, you would somehow increase your devotion. I do not think you should ever do such a thing when contemplating. Instead, take the words in their entirety. By "sin," understand the whole lump of it and connect it with nothing but yourself. I think this instinctive awareness of sin, imagined as a lump and identified with nothing but yourself, should make you the maddest person on earth and even in need of restraint! Whoever looks at you, however, would not think it by your appearance: sober in countenance, giving nothing away in your expressions, sitting, walking, lying, leaning, standing, or kneeling, wherever you are, in perfect calm!

Entering the Cloud

- *Do you understand how prayer for the contemplative differs from those in the beginning or proficient stages of the spiritual life?*

- *Do you see that the movement from purgation to virtue to mystical union with God involves a dependence on reading, meditative prayer, and then a deeper penetration into the mystery of the Godhead which asks the contemplative to let go of these venerable spiritual helps?*

- *Do you think that the contemplative must let go of them completely? What does the author say?*

- *Have you ever felt led to drop the traditional practices of reading, reflection, and discursive prayer to simply rest in God without thinking or saying anything? If so, where were you? What was it like? What can you remember of the experience? Is it something that simply happened? Is it something you have been able to do with some regularity? Did the experience change you in any way?*

- *Do you feel called to contemplation? Do you feel called to a life of pure contemplation? What is the difference?*

- *Where is God leading you at this point in your life?*

Chapter Thirty-Seven

*The special prayers of those who follow this book
and contemplate continually.*

Background

In this chapter, the author takes a deeper look into the prayer of
someone called to a life of pure contemplation, that is, one called
to enter and penetrate the cloud of unknowing by continually
opening one's heart to the impulse of divine love. He begins by
saying that, although such a person will have the deepest regard
for the official prayers of the Church and will use them with the
deepest care and utmost respect, his private prayers are another
matter. These are directed straight to God without the mediation
of any third party, be it a sacrament or a special intercessor such
as an angel, saint, or Church representative. These prayers come as
sudden intuitions and involve few if any words. Those words used
are usually very short and arise directly from the heart without
any previous reflection or analysis and should be understood as
a response to the inspiration of the Spirit. To help us understand
his message, he uses the example of someone trapped in a building suddenly engulfed by flames and who cries out, "Fire!" or
"Get out!" Such a cry will strike the ears of those in the vicinity
and alert them to the danger. In a similar way, a single word of
love—be it spoken or remaining only in thought—arising from
the depths of one's heart without previous thought or reflection
will penetrate the dark cloud of unknowing and reach the ears of
God in a thunderous clash. Such short, intense, passionate prayers
are inspired by the Spirit and are more likely to pierce the cloud
of unknowing than a long psalm recited poorly, with little attention and little regard for the Divine Being to whom it is addressed.

TEXT

JUST as the meditations of those who persevere through grace in this work of contemplation rise suddenly without intermediary means, so do their prayers. I am referring here to their private prayers, not to those designated by Holy Church. For true contemplatives revere such prayers so much that they follow them according to the form and statute ordained by the holy fathers before us. Their private prayers, however, rise spontaneously to God, without any intermediary means or prior meditation.

If they involve words (as they seldom do), they are few in number—in fact, the fewer the better. If it is a little word of one syllable, it is better than one of two and more in accordance with the work of the Spirit. For a true contemplative should always live at the highest, most spiritual peak. We can see this by looking at nature. A man or a woman suddenly frightened by fire or death or the like is suddenly driven by haste and needs to cry and beg after help. And how does he do it? Surely not in many words or even in a single word of two syllables. Why is that? Because he thinks it wastes too much time. To declare his urgent need, he bursts out in fear and cries out a single, one-syllable word such as "Fire!" or "Out!"

Just as this little word "fire" stirs and pierces the ears of the hearers, so does a single word of one syllable when it is not only spoken or thought but also expresses what lies in the "depths" of the spirit, which is the same as "height," for in spiritual matters, height, depth, length, and breadth are all the same. And it pierces the ears of Almighty God more than any long psalm mouthed without thought. And so it is written, "The short prayer pierces heaven."

Entering the Cloud

- *Do you draw a distinction between the Church's official worship (for example, Mass, the sacraments, the Liturgy of the Hours) and your own personal prayer life? How are they different? In what ways are they connected?*

- *What puts the official prayer of the Church in a special category? Is it because it is the prayer of Christ and his mystical body?*

- *In personal, private prayer, why do you think short, passionate words or thoughts arising directly from the heart have the power to penetrate heaven more than longer discursive compositions?*

- *Is it a question merely of the passion and intensity with which we pray or because it is easier to maintain shorter prayers at such levels? Is it because these brief intuitions represent the work of the Spirit in our hearts and, once expressed, return immediately to their home in the Godhead?*

- *Do the author's insights in this chapter correspond to your experience?*

- *Have you ever lifted your heart to God in a brief and intense prayer that simply came out of you without any prior reflection?*

- *Do such prayers simply happen or can we create them and send them off at will? Are they the work of the Spirit or of human hands? In what sense can they be considered a little of both? In what sense can all prayer be considered the work of the Spirit?*

- *What distinguishes mystical prayer from the ordinary prayer of everyday life? What makes them similar?*

- *In what sense does all prayer have its origin and destiny in the mystery of the Godhead?*

Chapter Thirtyeight

How and why a short prayer pierces heaven.

Background

In this chapter, the author tells us why such brief and intense prayers penetrate the cloud of unknowing and enter heaven. He uses Paul's words from Ephesians 3:17 about the height, depth, length, and breadth of God's Word to explain. He tells us that short prayers can pierce the dark cloud surrounding us and reach the ears of God himself because, in them, we are able to offer the fullness of our spirits: the height and depth, the length and breadth of our deepest, most spiritual selves. In terms of height, that single word contains all the might of the spirit. In terms of depth, it contains all the faculties of the spirit. In terms of length, it cries out to God with the same passion and intensity, even if it could be experienced repeatedly over time. In terms of breadth, it extends itself to others and wants for them exactly what it wants for itself.

The author goes on to describe God with the same imagery. God's length is his eternity; his love is his breadth; his power is his height; and his wisdom is his depth. Through a single word, our spirits can experience in a brief moment something of what the saints see when they come face-to-face with the height and depth and breadth and length of the all-wise, all-loving, all-powerful, and ever-living God. While most of our prayers are mediated through others, these single words of deep heartfelt love are able to pierce heaven and experience God (albeit for a single moment in time) as the saints themselves see him.

The author again uses the example of shouting out the word "Fire!" or "Out!" when being surrounded by flames. Upon hearing such a word, he says, we would get up in the middle of the night and be willing to help even our greatest enemy escape the flames. He concludes that we should expect much more from God who, upon hearing a single word expressed by the height and depth and length and breadth of our spirits, will have mercy and compassion on us and draw us to himself. Indeed, we should expect to be shown even more compassion and mercy, since these belong to God's very nature.

Text

WHY does this short little prayer of one syllable pierce heaven? Surely because it is prayed in the fullness of spirit: in the height, depth, length, and breadth of the spirit of the person praying. It is in the height, for it is prayed with all the might of the spirit. It is in the depth, for this little syllable contains all the wisdom of the spirit. It is in the length, for if it always felt as it now feels, it would always cry to God as it now cries. It is in the breadth, for it wants everyone to have what it has.

At this time, the soul understands the teaching of St. Paul and all the saints—not completely, but partially and in a manner of speaking, as it is according to the life of contemplation—about the length, breadth, height and depth of the everlasting and all-loving, almighty, and all-knowing God. God's eternity is His length; His love is His breadth; His might is His height; and His wisdom is His deepness. No wonder a soul so conformed by grace into the image and likeness of God his maker is heard by God so soon! Yes, this is so even if it is a very sinful soul, who is, as it were, an enemy to God. If he through grace were to cry such a short syllable in the height, depth, length, and breadth of his spirit, his anguished cry to God would always be heard, and he would be helped by God.

Look at this example. If you hear your deadly enemy crying out in fear from the depths of his heart this little word "Fire!" or "Out!" without considering that he was your enemy, but from the pity in your heart, you would rise up, even on a midwinter's night, and help him to put out his fire or quiet and ease his distress. O Lord! Since grace can enable a man to show so much mercy and pity to his enemy despite his enmity, what pity and what mercy will God have for the spiritual cry of a soul coming from the height, depth, length, and breadth of his spirit! God has everything by nature that

138

man has by grace. And surely God will have much more mercy, incomparably more, since what is had by nature is closer to eternal things than what is had by grace.

Entering the Cloud

- *Are you accustomed to thinking of the spiritual world according to the dimensions of the material (that is, height depth, length, and breadth)?*

- *Do you find it easy or difficult to picture your spirit as having these dimensions? Do you find it easy or difficult to picture God as having these dimensions? Do you find this analogy helpful or distracting? Can you think of another way of explaining the author's message?*

- *Do you find the author's analogy of saving an enemy from burning flames when crying out "fire" a helpful way of understanding the way God acts toward us when we send out brief heartfelt prayers to him? What do these analogies convey? What do they fail to convey?*

- *To what extent is the author himself struggling with language to convey an experience that ultimately cannot be expressed?*

- *To what extent has he reached the limitations of language here? To what extent do you think he is conscious of it?*

- *Have you ever had an intense experience of God in a brief moment of prayer as he describes? How would you describe the experience?*

Chapter Thirtynine

How the perfect contemplative should pray;
what prayer is in itself; if one should pray in words
and, if so, which words are most fitting for prayer.

Background

In this chapter, the author looks at the prayer of the pure contemplative. He also speaks to us about the true nature of contemplative prayer and suggests two words we could use should such prayer become vocal. He begins by reminding us that the pure contemplative, someone who has experienced the ways of purgation and illumination and who is now walking the path of union with God, prays with the height, depth, length, and breadth of his spirit. Every dimension of our being, in other words, is immersed in God and yearns for God to be equally immersed in us. Although words are not necessary at this level of prayer (and can even become a distraction), the author reminds us that prayer is nothing but our reaching out to God to acquire what is good and to avoid what is evil.

For the contemplative, this means turning away from sin and reaching out to God on every level of our being. Building on this simple dynamic, he suggests that when necessary, contemplatives might use the word "sin" when seeking to avoid evil and the word "God" when seeking a deeper experiential union with God. To be sure, our spirits must be totally involved when we pray in this way. We must avoid all other thought and simply cry these simple words out to God in a spoken word, a single intense thought, or a passionate desire. He prizes these words above all others because they capture the essence of what our prayer is trying to attain. He warns us, however, not to try analyzing these words, for doing so will lead us away from the path of unknowing where God awaits us with his loving embrace. Since God comes to us not through deliberation but through grace, he bids us to put all thought aside and to use these words as a way of gathering our spirits into a passionate and loving impulse that will penetrate the cloud of unknowing and reach the dwelling place of God.

The author likes the words "sin" and "God" because they are brief and capture the very essence of prayer. At the same time, he offers them only as examples, since we ourselves must be drawn to the words we carry to God in contemplative prayer. Indeed, words themselves are not necessary for pure contemplation, although they may be used as a means of gathering our spirits and focusing all of our power and intensity on the one we seek. If we are drawn to them, they should be short and meaningful. What is more, we pray them again and again with the same heartfelt passion until we reach our goal. The author ends the chapter with a familiar image. We are to cry these words out to God without ceasing, just as a man in a burning building will not cease shouting out "Fire! Fire!" or "Out! Out!" until he and his friends have been rescued and brought to safety.

TEXT

AND so we must pray in the height, depth, length, and breadth of our spirit. Not with many words, but in a little word of one syllable. And what should this word be? Surely one suited to the nature of prayer. And what word is that? Let us first look at what prayer is in itself, and afterward we may see more clearly what word is best suited to the nature of prayer.

In itself, prayer is nothing but a devout movement of the will toward God in order to obtain good and remove evil. Since all evil is contained in sin, either by cause or nature, when we pray with the intention of getting rid of evil, we should not say, think, or intend anything other than this little word "sin." And if we intentionally pray for acquiring good, let us cry out, in word, thought, or desire nothing other than the word "God." For in God contains all good, both by cause and by being. Do not be surprised that I set these words before all others. If I could find any shorter words that contain in them so completely all good and all evil, as do these two words, or if I had been taught by God to take any other words, I would have taken them and left these behind. This is my advice to you.

Do not study these words. If you do, you will never arrive at your purpose or come to contemplation, which is not attained by study but by grace alone. Take no other words with you in prayer, despite all I have said here, other than those that God inspires you to use. Still, if God leads you to these, I advise you not to leave them if you are going to use words in your prayer (do not do so otherwise). They are very short words. Although short prayer is highly recommended here, the frequency of prayer should not decrease. As I have said before, it is prayed in the length of one's spirit and it will not stop until it fully attains what it longs for. Take the example of the terrified man or a woman we spoke of earlier. They never cease crying out this little word "Out!" or this little word "Fire!" until they have received all the help they need in their grief.

Entering the Cloud

- *Do you understand what lies at the essence of contemplative prayer? Do you understand what makes such prayer different from ordinary prayer? How would you explain this difference to a friend?*

- *Do you understand the reason for the author's allowance of words in contemplative prayer? Why must these words be short and prayed with intensity? How could such words inhibit a person's contemplation? How could they augment it and actually lead this person to God?*

- *In what way can a word lead us beyond itself? How can a word spoken in the throes of contemplation lead us to God?*

- *Do you pray in a contemplative manner?*

- *Do you use words when you pray in this way? What words are you drawn to? What do these words tell you about yourself? What do they not tell you? What do the words tell you about the mystery of God? What do they not tell you?*

Chapter Forty

In this work of contemplation, a soul gives no special attention to any particular vice or virtue.

Background

In this chapter, the author offers more instruction on how words such as "sin" and "God" should be used in contemplative prayer. For example, when uttering the word "sin" with all the might our spirits can muster, we must take care not to reflect on any particular sin or vice. Since all sins—of whatever type—separate us from God, contemplatives typically do not avert to the kind and measure of their offenses. For us, one sin is as serious as the next and must be condemned with the same fervor and intensity. What is more, pondering our growth (or lack thereof) in the moral life, while an important feature of the illuminative way, should cede to the background when we embark on the way of contemplation. Rather than using our powers of reflection to focus on particular sins and vices, we should try instead to experience a more basic understanding of the dreadful reality of sin in our lives.

The author bids us to look upon sin as a single, massive lump deep within us that is constantly working to turn our minds and hearts away from God. When our spirits cry out, "Sin, sin, sin!" and, "Out, out, out!" we should see ourselves as begging God to free us from these base, sinful tendencies. Such prayer, he tells us, is better learned directly from God himself, who teaches us through his grace and the promptings of his Spirit. As with the word "sin," he likewise encourages contemplatives to utter the word "God" in a similarly pure and single-hearted way. Rather than being concerned about special works or virtues, we should instead be concerned simply with fostering an intimate relationship with God himself. The author encourages us to cry out from the depths of our hearts by mustering all the might of our spirits in this single word so we have nothing in our hearts but the desire for God himself. He goes on to say that, at this point in our spiritual journey, we need not worry any longer about growth in the virtues, since an authentic mystical experience of God will carry such growth in its wake. He concludes by saying that the contemplative prayer involves a continual movement back and forth between words such as "sin" and "God" and is accompanied by a sense of their antithetical presence in our lives during our earthly sojourn.

TEXT

IN the same manner, you should fill your heart with the spiritual meaning of the word "Sin" and care not if it is venial or mortal, or pride, anger, envy, avarice, sloth, gluttony, or lust. What concern is it to contemplatives what kind of sin it is or how great it is? For when they are engaged in contemplation, they think all sins are great because they separate them from God and disturb their spiritual peace.

Feel sin in its entirety, as a great lump, within you, without worrying about its details. Then cry continually in your spirit this one thing: "Sin, sin, sin! Out, out, out!" This spiritual cry is better learned from God by experience than from any man by word. It is best when it is entirely spiritual, unuttered and with no premeditation. At times, an abundance of spirit will burst out into words because your body and soul overflow with sorrow and the heaviness of sin.

In the same manner, you should also use the little word "God." Fill your heart with its spiritual meaning, without considering any of His individual works: whether they are good, better, or best of all; whether they are bodily or spiritual; or whether they are virtues wrought in man's soul by grace, and in this last case without determining if it be humility or charity, patience or abstinence, hope, faith, or soberness, chastity or voluntary poverty. What does all this matter to contemplatives? For they find and experience in God all virtues. In Him all things exist both by cause and by being. They know that if they have God they have all that is good, and so they desire nothing in particular, but only the good God. Do the same, as far as you can by grace, and consider God everything, and everything God so that nothing operates in your mind and will but God alone.

And because while you live this wretched life you will always feel in some way this foul, stinking lump of sin as one with the substance of your being, you must continually return to these two words: "Sin" and "God." Know that if you had God, you would not have sin, and if you had no sin, you would have God.

Entering the Cloud

- *Why does the author warn contemplatives not to think about the nature of their sins and good works or of the scope of their vices and virtues? Does it have something to do with the nature of contemplative prayer itself?*

- *Would such reflections be a hindrance to what God is trying to achieve in them through intense single-word prayers such as "sin" and "God," which are meant to gather the might of their spirits and repeatedly pound against the cloud of unknowing?*

- *How can such prayers hope to penetrate heaven if they are continually weighed down by more diffuse reflections of lesser intensity?*

- *Do you agree that a contemplative should pray to God using few (if any) words that, when uttered, should be spontaneous outbursts that muster all the power and might of their spirits toward heaven?*

- *Have you ever prayed in this way? Would you like to pray in this way? Have you ever asked God to help you?*

Chapter Forty-one

Discretion applies everywhere else but here.

Background

In this chapter, the author tells us that, while all other activities in our lives require moderation, the practice for penetrating the cloud of unknowing knows no excess. Seeking the "Golden Mean" between excess and defect—what the Desert Fathers and the monastic tradition they inspired called "discretion" and the Greek philosophers and medieval scholastics, "prudence"—lies at the very heart of the Christian ascetical tradition. According to this understanding of the moral life, every virtue involves steering clear of its two contrary vices: one that goes into excess; the other, into defect. The author tells us that the prayer he has been suggesting for penetrating the cloud of unknowing is not bound by this otherwise steadfast Christian "rule of thumb." On the contrary, he insists that there should be no holding back when it comes to knocking on the cloud of unknowing with the impulse of love. His reason for saying so is because the goal of this practice is not the acquisition of virtue as such, but something far greater: the face-to-face experience of God himself. To possess God in an authentic mystical experience is the ultimate goal of the Christian life and presupposes the presence of the virtues in our lives.

The author wishes we could pray this prayer at all times, if not in actual practice, then at least in our desire. He recognizes that illness and bodily weakness can, at times, hinder our practice of this intense form of prayer. Because good health helps us in such prayer, he tells us to take good care of ourselves so that we will have the necessary stamina and strength for it. He tells us to do our utmost to avoid illness and anything that could contribute to our physical weakness and thus interfere with this special practice. When sickness does come our way, however, he bids us to humbly

146

and patiently place ourselves in God's merciful hands, for such trials have much to teach us and can be more pleasing to God than any other prayer or spiritual devotion.

TEXT

FURTHERMORE, if you were to ask me how much discretion you should exercise in this work, I would say, "None at all!" In all your other activities, such as eating, drinking, sleeping, keeping warm or cool, praying, reading, and conversing with your fellow Christians, you must use your discretion. In all these, you must exercise discretion so that there is neither too much nor too little. In this work, however, keep no control, for I want you to keep doing it for as long as you live.

I am not saying that you will always come to it fresh, for that is impossible. At times, sickness, some other imbalances of body and soul, or natural necessities will hinder you and often draw you down from the height of contemplation. But you should always work at it, either in practice or in intention. For God's sake, beware of sickness as much as you can so that as far as possible you will not be the cause of your weakness. For I tell you the truth when I say this work requires much peace and a pure and complete disposition in body and soul.

So for God's sake, govern yourself well in body and in soul, and stay as healthy as you can. If sickness comes anyway, be patient and wait humbly for God's mercy. That is enough. For I tell you the truth when I say that patience in sickness and in other difficulties pleases God much more than any happy devotion you may have when healthy.

Entering the Cloud

- *Do you agree that "discretion" or "prudence," taken in the sense of finding the mean between extremes, will help you grow in virtue?*

- *What is specifically Christian about such a belief? Does it have to do with the power of grace to transform our humanity, even our powers for virtuous action?*

- *In what sense have the monastic and scholastic traditions "baptized" an understanding of virtue already deeply rooted in the Western philosophical tradition?*

- *Why does the author insist that the particular discipline of prayer he promotes is not bound to the rule of the mean between two extremes?*

- *Is he calling this principle of virtuous action into question or simply giving us some perspective on it?*

- *Why does he insist that we can never practice his discipline of prayer to excess? Does this apply to all prayer or only to the prayer of pure contemplatives?*

- *Do you agree with his belief that poor health can hinder the way we pray? Have you ever experienced this in your own life? Is it possible to offer up an illness or human handicap as a prayer to God?*

Chapter Forty-two

Through a lack of discretion in contemplation, we become discreet in everything else—and surely in no other way.

Background

In this chapter, the author tells us we can achieve moderation in all things (for example, eating, drinking, sleeping, etc.) if we but devote ourselves unceasingly (and without moderation) to the practice of pure contemplation. He is convinced we will find the proper balance—the mean between excess and defect—in all we think, say, and do, if we but focus our hearts passionately on penetrating the cloud of unknowing with the spiritual exercise of simply crying out "Sin! Sin!" whenever we wish to avoid evil and "God! God!" whenever we wish to draw near to God. He understands that this may not make much rational sense, so he bids us simply to accept this teaching as best we can. In his mind, all we need to do is devote ourselves day and night to this simple exercise and all else will fall into its proper place. He finds it difficult to believe that anything else could happen to those who abandon themselves to God in this way. He goes on to say that, immersed in this dark impulse of love, we would be so enamored of God that we would not even stop to think about such things as eating and drinking. We would perform these natural outward activities when necessary, with perfect moderation, and with little if any reflection, while our minds all the while would be focused on the one thing that matters: union with the Godhead. Although he recognizes that others may have different opinions about the virtuous life and its relationship to prayer, he insists that the dark path into the cloud of unknowing gives authentic witness rooted in sound human experience to what it means to live "the good life."

TEXT

PERHAPS you will ask me how you should govern yourself discreetly in food and in sleep and in all these other things. My answer is short: "Take what you receive!" Do this work of contemplation without ceasing and without discretion every day and you will know well enough when to begin and cease in all other works with great discretion. I cannot believe that a soul who continues night and day without discretion in this work of contemplation would err in any of these outward activities. If he does, I think he is the kind of person who would always err.

And so if I am able to give complete and undivided attention to this spiritual work within in my soul, I would then be indifferent about eating, drinking, sleeping, speaking, or any of my outward activities. I would rather come to discretion concerning them through such indifference than by giving them my close attention and controlling them by mark and measure. Indeed, I could never bring it about in this manner, regardless of what I say or do. Let others say what they will. Allow experience to testify. So lift up your heart with a blind stirring of love and consider now "sin" and now "God." You want to have God and you want to lose sin. God wants you, and you know what sin is. May the good God help you now, for now you have need of Him!

Entering the Cloud

- *Do you agree that there is an intimate connection between the way of virtue and the way of contemplation?*

- *Do you agree that we can achieve moderation in all things simply by focusing our attention entirely on God with simple, heartfelt prayers that pierce heaven with all the gathered strength of our spirits?*

- *Do you see any dangers in the author's approach to the acquisition of virtue? Is he replacing one approach to virtue with another or simply offering an alternative means? Is his approach to virtue meant for everyone or only for a select few?*

- *What has been your experience of the way of virtue and the way of prayer?*

- *What has been your experience of the way of virtue and the way of contemplation?*

Chapter Forty-three

All knowledge and experience of one's own being must be lost if
the perfection of this work is to be truly experienced in this life.

Background

In this chapter, the author tells us of the contemplative's need to cast awareness of all things other than God into the cloud of forgetting. This holds true for all created things, their activities, and the way they impact the understanding and will. It also holds true for all self-knowledge, including all thoughts, desires, feelings, and actions. If we wish to penetrate the cloud of unknowing, we must not allow any creaturely knowledge whatsoever to stand between us and God. This includes even our own self-consciousness and the experience of our own existence.

The perfect love of God, the author tells us, means not only loving God above all things but even denying ourselves for his sake. We must consider all things undesirable and even loathsome if they stand between us and the object of our love. This holds true especially for own selves. The only way to do away with such knowledge and feelings is to cast them into the cloud of forgetting. This task of complete forgetting is required of all who wish to penetrate the cloud of unknowing and enter into union with the Godhead. The author goes so far as to say that we must do away with even the simple awareness and feeling of our own being. To truly love ourselves, in other words, we must be willing to forget ourselves completely. We must deny ourselves on every level in order to be embraced by the eternal love of the Godhead.

TEXT

SEE to it that nothing operates in your mind or will but God alone. Try to stamp out all knowledge and feeling of all things but God and trample them down under the cloud of forgetting. In this work of contemplation, you are to forget not only all creatures other than yourself (their deeds as well as your own) but also yourself and even the deeds you have done for God. For a perfect lover must not only love what he loves more than himself but also hate himself for the sake of what he loves.

You must do so with yourself. You must loathe and be wary of all that occupies your mind and will unless it is God. For nothing else, whatever it is, may come between you and God. No wonder you loathe and hate thinking of yourself when you always feel your sin to be a foul, stinking lump between you and God. For the lump is nothing else than yourself. For you think of it as inseparable from you and one with the substance of your being.

Break up your knowledge and experience of all creaturely things, especially of yourself. Your knowledge and experience of all things depends on your own self-knowledge and experience. Along with this self-knowledge and experience, everything else is quickly forgotten. If you wish to test it, you will find that when you have forgotten all other creatures and all their works—and all your own works as well—there will still remain between you and God a naked knowledge and experience of your own being. You must destroy even this awareness and feeling before you can reach perfect contemplation.

Entering the Cloud

- *Why must we cast all things into the cloud of forgetting in order to penetrate the cloud of unknowing? Is such forgetting even humanly possible?*

- *How can we purge our memory of all its feeling and content? What would such a cleansing or purgation do to us?*

- *Who would we be without our memories?*

- *Can we achieve this state of forgetting on our own? To what extent do we need God's help?*

- *Is it possible for us to forget the simple awareness and feeling of our being?*

- *Do you believe all things are possible with God?*

Chapter Forty-four

*How a soul must dispose itself to destroy all knowledge
and experience of its own being.*

Background

In this chapter, the author tells us that doing away with the naked
knowledge of our being occurs only through a special grace from
God and a corresponding capacity to receive it. Losing consciousness of our being does away with all other obstacles to penetrating
the cloud of unknowing and seeing God face-to-face. He goes
on to describe the capacity for receiving this special grace as a
deep spiritual sorrow experienced in the depths of a stillness that
resembles sleep and makes all other sorrows seem like a dream.
This perfect sorrow purifies our souls of sin and frees us from the
temporal punishment they incur. It also fills us with holy longings
and prepares us for the joy that comes from forgetting our own
beings and losing ourselves completely in God.

Without this perfect sorrow, we would not be able to be elevated
by God beyond the experience of our own beings. Without it, we
would continue to experience ourselves as nothing but a putrid
lump of sin. Were we not empowered by God to forget our very
existence and be consoled by the bountiful nature of his transforming grace, we would be overcome by the knowledge of our
deep sinfulness and corruption. Even though we have overcome
the knowledge and experience of our own existence, however, we
never wish simply to cease to be. Such a desire would show hatred
for God and be the manifest work of the evil one. On the contrary,
we rejoice in our existence and give heartfelt thanks to God for the
gift of being. We must experience this deep and total sorrow if we
wish to be perfectly united to God, insofar as it is possible in this
life. We must look to God to bestow it as he sees fit and according
to his good pleasure.

154

TEXT

YOU ask me how you can destroy this naked knowledge and experience of your own being. If it were destroyed, you may be thinking that all other difficulties would also be destroyed. And you would be right. Still, my answer is that, without a special grace freely given by God and your own capacity and willingness to receive it, this naked knowledge and experience of your being cannot possibly be destroyed. And this capacity is nothing else than an intensely deep spiritual sorrow.

But in this sorrow you need to exercise discretion. During the time of this sorrow, you must be wary of overburdening your body and spirit. Instead, sit quite still, as if you were asleep, fully absorbed and sunken in sorrow. This is true, perfect sorrow, and all will go well if you achieve this kind of sorrow. Everyone has some reason for sorrow, but no one more who knows and feels that he is. All other sorrow in comparison with this is an imitation of the real thing. For he experiences true sorrow who knows and feels not only what he is but that he is. Let him who has never felt this sorrow be sorry indeed, for he has not yet experienced perfect sorrow. This sorrow, when we have it, cleanses the soul not only of sin but also of the suffering caused by sin. And it makes the soul capable of receiving the joy we have when we lose all knowledge and experience of our existence.

When authentic, such sorrow is full of holy desire. Without such desire, no one on earth could bear it. For were the soul not fed and comforted by its good endeavors, it would not be able to withstand the pain of the knowledge and experience of his own being. For as often as he would have a true knowledge and experience of God in the purity of his heart (as much as it is possible here) and then feels he may not (for he finds his knowledge and experience so occupied and filled with the foul stinking lump of himself, which must always be hated, despised, and forsaken, if he would be God's perfect disciple, as the Lord Himself taught on the Mount of Perfection), just as often, he goes nearly mad with sorrow. So much so that he weeps and wails, strives, curses, and denounces himself. Simply stated, he thinks the burden he bears is so heavy that he does not care what befalls him so long as God is pleased. Yet in all this sorrow he does not want to cease existing, for that would be the devil's madness and contempt of God. Though he continues longing to be free of this awareness, he wants very much to go on existing, and he gives God heartfelt thanks for this precious gift.

Every soul must know and experience this sorrow and longing in one form or other. God teaches His spiritual disciples according to His good will and their capacity in body and soul, in degree and disposition, before they can be perfectly united with Him in perfect love, as far as it is earthly possible, and if God permits.

Entering the Cloud

- *Why does losing consciousness of our naked being depend on God's grace rather than on human effort? Is there any way we can prepare ourselves for this grace?*

- *Why must we also have the capacity to receive this grace for it to carry out its work in us? Is this capacity to receive also something given to us by God?*

- *What does the author mean by perfect sorrow? How does it differ from other human sorrows?*

- *Why is it necessary to experience it before we can lose the simple awareness of our existence?*

- *Have you ever experienced the simple sense of your own being? Have you ever lost this simple awareness?*

- *Have you ever experienced perfect sorrow? If not, have you asked for it?*

- *Have you ever felt so lost in God that you lost awareness of your own existence?*

Chapter Forty-five

A detailed account of some of the deceptions that may happen in this work.

Background

In this chapter, the author points out some of the mistakes we can make in our attempt to follow the path of pure contemplation. These illusions can easily befall those of us who are just starting out on this path and have little experience in the practices being suggested. For this reason, he wants beginners in the contemplative life to receive sound spiritual direction to help them discern the true path of contemplation from the false. Pride, sensuality, and false reasoning are what usually lie behind the various missteps to which we succumb at this early stage. One mistake would be taking the notion of lifting our hearts up to God without ceasing too literally. Rather than raising our hearts to God in a spiritual sense, we focus our minds on trying to raise our physical, carnal hearts higher up in the chest cavity. This misapplication of the spiritual practice results in our becoming both physically and mentally exhausted. We become weary in both body and soul and then become easy prey to temptation promising sensual, bodily pleasure.

Other dangers are due, if not to spiritual blindness or the improper way we treat our bodies, to an unnatural spiritual passion or a false heat in the imagination that comes from the evil one. If we are not careful, we can mistake these experiences as a fire of love produced by the grace of the Holy Spirit and end up falling prey to great hypocrisy, heresy, and error. The author points out that the evil one is a master of disguise (an "angel of light" so to speak) who has his own contemplatives, just as God has. He says there are many different kinds of illusions and deceits that can befall us and that each state of life has its own particular variations. The possibilities of deception are as vast and as varied as the possibilities for good for those in a healthy state of contemplation. Here, he wishes to focus simply on those illusions that the reader will most likely encounter and guard against with special care.

TEXT

LET me tell you this. In this work of contemplation, a young disciple, inexperienced and unproven in spiritual matters, may be deceived. Unless he is cautious and has the grace to stop what he is doing and receives counsel with humility, he may be physically destroyed and become prey to spiritual fantasies. All this is because he is proud, materialistic, and overly inquisitive.

He could be deceived in this way. Young men and women just beginning in the school of devotion hear someone read or speak about this sorrow and longing. They hear how a person should lift his heart to God and constantly long to experience the love of God. And immediately in their curious minds they understand these words not in their intended spiritual sense but in a material and physical one, and they overly exert their physical hearts in their breasts! And because they are without grace and are proud and inquisitive, they strain their veins and their bodily powers in such a wild and unruly way that within a short time they fall into frenzies, weariness, and a feebleness in body and in soul. This causes them to turn away from the inner life and to seek some false and empty material and bodily comforts from without, under the pretense of recreation for body and spirit. Or, if they do not do this, they develop from their spiritual blindness and the physical irritation in their bodily breasts caused by the pretended work of the spirit (which is, in fact, animal) a natural glow within caused by the abuse of their bodies or their hollow beliefs. Or else they experience a false heat wrought by the fiend, their spiritual enemy, on account of their pride, materialism, and inquisitiveness. And they may imagine it to be the fire of love, lighted and kindled by the grace and goodness of the Holy Spirit. From this deceit many evils spring: much hypocrisy and heresy and error. For very soon, after the arrival of this false feeling comes a false knowledge in the school of the fiend, just as true experience is followed by true knowledge in the school of God. For I tell you truly that the devil has his contemplatives, as God has His.

Such deceitful and false experience and this false knowledge have as many diverse and astonishing varieties as there are different states of life and personal temperaments to be deceived. So too have the true experiences and knowledge of the saved. But I will put down here no more spiritual lies than those I think will assail you if you ever intend to become a contemplative. For how does it profit you to know how clergy and men and women of different backgrounds from your own are deceived? Certainly in no way whatsoever. So I am telling you no more than those that will happen to you if you undertake this work of contemplation. And I tell you this so that you will be wary if they should assail you on the way.

Entering the Cloud

- *To what illusions or self-deceptions have you become prey to during your life? How did you succumb to them? How did you discover that they were leading you astray?*

- *How did you get back on the right track? Did you go by any basic rules of thumb?*

- *How might a spiritual director have helped?*

- *If the evil one is a master of deception, what can you do to protect yourself against his advances?*

- *What spiritual illusions are peculiar to your state in life?*

- *What more can you do to overcome pride, sensuality, and false reasoning?*

- *What more can you do to help you determine whether something is from God or the evil one?*

Chapter Forty-Six

*How to escape such deceptions; the work of contemplation
demands a zealous spirit rather than bodily austerities.*

Background

In this chapter, the author tells us how we can avoid some of the
pitfalls that lead beginners in the contemplative way astray. He
reminds us that penetrating the cloud of unknowing is not a matter
of bodily strength but of spiritual disposition. Rather than exerting ourselves physically, we should foster humility and patience in
our hearts and allow God's plan to gradually unfold in our lives.
Contemplative (or mystical) union is a work of grace, not of human effort. If we find ourselves trying to cause it in some way, we
may end up fooling ourselves into thinking that we have power
over God and can somehow control his actions through our own.

The results are even worse, the author goes onto say, if we think
we can do so through physical effort. In such a case, we demean
the divine by trying to bring it down to the level of brute animal
strength. To offset these pitfalls, he asks us simply to wait with
patience for God's will to manifest itself in our lives and to do
so with humility and respect. These spiritual attitudes are themselves divine gifts and will prepare our hearts for God to work
in them. The author encourages us to enter into a kind of game
with God whereby we try to keep from him how much we truly
desire to see and experience him. Playing with God in this way is
not a sign of disrespect but something that highlights God's love
for us—and vice versa. Just as a father plays with his child with
kisses and loving embraces, so we must be willing to receive God's
love as it is manifested in the circumstances of our lives. Playfully
hiding our thoughts and feelings from God—a kind of spiritual
peekaboo—reveals a level of comfort and trust that is otherwise
difficult to express.

160

Text

SO for the love of God, be cautious in this matter and do not exert your heart beyond your strength. Work with zealous pleasure instead of raw strength. For the more zealous your work, the more humble and spiritual it will become; the cruder, the more material and animal. So be wary. For the animal heart that dares to touch the summit of contemplation will be beaten away with stones. [18] Stones are hard, dry, and hurt when they hit. Such violent blows are inseparable from a materialistic and physical outlook and are dry for the lack of the dew of grace. They sorely hurt the foolish soul as it festers in illusions made by fiends. So beware of behaving with such beastly rudeness and learn to love joyfully with quiet, demure behavior, at peace in both body and soul. Abide the will of our Lord courteously and humbly. Do not snatch at it like a greedy greyhound, however much you hunger for it. If I may employ an amusing example, do all you can to conceal your immense and unruly spiritual longing, as if you were altogether unwilling that He should know how very glad you would be to see Him, have Him, and feel Him.

Perhaps you think I am speaking childishly and playfully. I believe that whoever has the grace to do and feel as I say will have a delightful spiritual game to play with God, who will hug and kiss him as a father does his child, as He so enjoys.

Entering the Cloud

- *Do you agree that contemplative (or mystical) union with God is completely a matter of divine grace?*

- *Have you ever felt yourself working too hard at such union, as if it were a matter of your own effort? What other pitfalls or obstacles have you experienced in your attempt to walk the way of contemplation?*

- *Why are patience and humility so important for the spiritual life? Why are they so important for contemplative union with God?*

- *Have you ever thought of your spiritual journey as a kind of play? What are the strengths of such a metaphor? How could such a metaphor be misunderstood? Can you think of any other metaphors for describing contemplative union with the divine?*

- *What is your favorite metaphor for describing your relationship with God? What are its strengths and weaknesses? In what sense do all metaphors limp when they seek to express the relationship between the human and the divine?*

Chapter Forty-Seven

A teaching on purity of spirit required by this work of contemplation; how the soul should reveal its desire to God and to man in a different way.

Background

In this chapter, the author reveals why we should hide the deepest desires of our hearts from God. For one thing, he believes that doing so will actually make what we are hiding clearer to God, since the knowledge we are conveying is not tainted by the sensible world. Because God is pure spirit and man is a composite of body and soul, each requires from us a different way of disclosing what lies deep within us. Concealing our deepest desires from God in the playful manner suggested in the last chapter allows us to reveal, by way of concealment, a mode of self-disclosure very different from our normal conversational, image- and thought-based means of communication. This way of concealment moves us away from the familiar realm of sensible feeling into that of the spiritual. It enables us, moreover, to tie a spiritual knot with God that unites our wills in love, making us spiritually one.

The author believes that, when mixed with elements of the natural order (for instance, words, images, and thought), the knowledge we are seeking to convey is compromised and does not convey the same depth of spiritual knowledge as the way of concealment. Even though we already know we cannot hide anything from God (hence the element of play or gaming), this imageless and thoughtless way of concealed showing is considered the most authentic means of self-disclosure we can have with God. Since God is purely spiritual, we must strive when revealing our deepest selves to him to remove all signs of sensible reality. We must present him, in a sense, with our own cloud of unknowing and allow him to penetrate our inner darkness and ultimately the depths of our hearts. Since we often have mixed motivations for doing things and since we ourselves can be unaware of our own deepest desires, the way of concealment represents the purest and most complete way possible for us to disclose ourselves to the divine.

TEXT

DO NOT be surprised that I speak so childishly, and, as it were, foolishly and lacking natural discretion. I do so for certain reasons, and since I think I have been moved for some time to feel, think, and speak this way to some of my other special friends in God, I do so now to you.

One reason why I tell you to conceal from God the desire of your heart is because I think—to your profit and the fulfillment of your desire—your hope would come to his attention more easily by concealing it rather than by revealing it in any other manner. Another reason is because by such a "hidden revelation" I want to get you out of the volatility of bodily emotions into the purity and depth of spiritual experience, ultimately to help you to knit the spiritual knot of burning love between yourself and God, in spiritual unity and conformity of will.

You know very well that God is a Spirit and that whoever wishes be made one with Him must be authentic in depth of spirit, far from any bodily pretense. It is true that God knows all things and that nothing physical or spiritual can be kept from Him. Since He is a spirit, however, what is hidden in the depths of a man's spirit is to Him even more clearly known and obvious than what is mixed with the physical. For physical things are naturally farther from God than spiritual things. For this reason, when our desire is mingled with anything physical (as it is when we stress and strain ourselves in both body and spirit), it is farther from God than it would be if it were done with more devotion and more sober eagerness, purity, and depth of spirit.

Here you may see, at least in part, the reason why I tell you so childishly to cover and hide your burning longing from God. Still, I do not tell you to hide it completely, for it would be the counsel of a fool to tell you to do something that cannot be done. But I tell you to do what you can to hide it. I tell you this because I want you to cast it into the depths of your soul, far from any mingling with the physical that would make it less spiritual and farther from God. Also, because I know that the more spiritual your soul becomes, the less earthly its desires will be, the nearer will it be to God, the more it will please Him, and the more clearly it will be noticeable to Him. Not that He sees anything more clearly at one time than at another—for He does not change—but because it is more like Him, when it is pure in spirit, for He is a Spirit.

There is another reason why I tell you to do your best not to let Him know. You and I, and many like us, are liable to understand spiritual things in material terms. Had I asked you to show God the movement of your heart, you may have expressed it physically by gesture, voice, word, or in some other bodily way, in the same way that you show what is in your inmost heart to a friend. To this extent, your action would have been a mixed one. For we reveal something to a man in one way and to God in another.

Entering the Cloud

- *Why does the author insist we must keep our deepest desires hidden from God? Is it possible to do so if we ourselves are unaware of them? Does this type of self-disclosure presuppose a certain level of human and Christian maturity?*

- *Does the author's notion of concealed disclosure even make sense to you? Does it need to? What aspects of it do you find hard to grasp?*

- *Do you get a sense that the author is speaking from his own experience? To whom is he talking? To whom is he not talking?*

- *How would you describe the playful, gaming side of this practice? What dangers are involved in it? Have you ever tried to relate to God in this way?*

- *In what ways is self-disclosure through concealed disclosure different from the ordinary ways of Christian prayer? How is it different from other ways of Christian mysticism? In what sense can all Christian prayer be considered a type of play?*

Chapter Forty-eight

*God wants us to serve Him with body and soul and reward
us in both; how we shall know when all those sounds
and delights that come to the body during prayer are good
and when they are evil.*

Background

In this chapter, the author provides some context for his insights
on concealed disclosure that should help us integrate it more easily
into his overall teaching. To begin with, he does not mean to give
the impression that contemplatives should never speak to God with
words coming straight from the heart. Short, passionate darts of fire
like, "Good Jesus! Lovely Jesus! Sweet Jesus!" can arise spontaneously from deep within our hearts and achieve bodily expression
that is good and holy. Nor does he wish to give the impression that
he is in some way trying to separate body and soul. He reminds
us that we are composite creatures and that, despite the dangers
we face in this fallen world, God will reward us at times with deep
spiritual experiences involving both body and soul.

The author acknowledges that God can set our bodily senses
ablaze with deep consolations that come from an overflow of spiritual gladness arising from deep within us. Whenever they occur,
we should not hold these experiences suspect but welcome them
as gratuitous gifts from God. Other bodily consolations, however,
come from outside of us and must be put to the test because they
can be either good or bad, depending on their point of origin. We
must strip these of all false reasoning. To help with this process,
he points to his own instructions in the previous chapters and
the useful insight of others, should we find them. Once carefully
scrutinized and found to be free of all evil, these outward consolations are to be readily received as coming directly from God
without any intermediary. He does not go any further into how to

166

discern whether these consolations come from God, saying that it is treated much better in another book. Although he does not name this book specifically, it seems likely that he is referring to Walter Hilton's The Scale of Perfection (1:8–12). As for his own insights on the matter, he simply asks us to put those consolations coming through the window of the senses to the test. Because they can be either good or evil, he bids us to stir our hearts with the simple, devout, and passionate impulse of love. Even if we are not sure of their origin at the outset, this impulse will bind up our hearts against evil and eventually give us the assurance we need either inwardly from the Spirit of God or outwardly from the wise counsel of a spiritual director.

TEXT

I SAY this not because I want you to stop praying vocally whenever you are so moved or to prevent you from bursting forth in an overflow of spiritual devotion in normal speech with some good words such as, "Good Jesus!" "Fair Jesus!" "Sweet Jesus!"—and the like. No, God forbid you take it in this way! For I really do not mean this. God forbid that I should divide what he has joined, the body and spirit. For God wants to be served with body and soul, both together, as is right, and to give man his heavenly reward in body as well as soul. And as a foretaste of that reward, He will sometimes enflame the body of His devout servants in this life: not once or twice but sometimes often, and when He likes, with very wonderful delights and consolations. Not all of this comes into our bodies from without through the windows of our mind; they also come from within, rising and springing from the abundance of true spiritual gladness and devotion. Such comfort and sweetness should not be held suspect, and in short, I believe that whoever experiences it cannot regard it so.

Please suspect all other comforts, sounds, gladness, and delights of unknown origin that come suddenly to you from without. For they can be good or evil: the work of a good angel if good and of an evil angel if evil. They will not be evil if their curious deceits of knowledge and strain on the heart are removed as I have suggested, or in better ways if you know them. And why? Surely because the reason for this comfort is a devout movement of love dwelling in a pure spirit. It is wrought by the hand of Almighty God, directly in the soul. It must therefore always be free from whatever fantasy or false opinion a person may acquire in this life.

Of the other comforts, sounds, and delights, and how you can know whether they be good or evil, I will not tell you at this time. Not because I think it unnecessary but because you can find it written in another place in another's work a thousand times better than I can say or write. You can find all that I set out here dealt with far better there. But what of it? I shall not cease from, nor tire of, seeking to meet the desires and movements of your heart that you have shown you possess first in your words and now in your deeds.

I will say only this about those sounds and delights that come in through the windows of your mind and which may be good or evil. Practice continually this blind, devout, and eager stirring of love I speak of and I have no doubt it will be quite capable of telling you about them itself. Even if you are astonished when they first come, because you are not accustomed to them, it will nevertheless bind your heart so well that you will never give full great credence to them until you are absolutely sure through the inner approval of the Spirit of God or from without through counsel of a discreet spiritual father.

Entering the Cloud

- *Do the author's words in this chapter clarify his teaching on concealed disclosure?*

- *Do you understand his desire to affirm the body-soul unity, while at the same time reminding us of the present dangers of the physical, sensible world?*

- *Why does the author encourage us to embrace those short passionate prayers that arise spontaneously within our hearts?*

- *Do you agree that spiritual and bodily consolations can come to us directly from God from deep within our hearts?*

- *Do you agree that they can also come to us outwardly through the window of the senses? Which does the author prefer? Which must we hold suspect and carefully put to the test? Which have you experienced?*

- *At this point in your life, does God help you to discern good and evil directly through the promptings of his Spirit or more indirectly through the counsel of others? Does he speak to you perhaps through both? Which do you prefer?*

Chapter Forty-nine

*The substance of all perfection is nothing other than a good will;
how all sounds, comforts and delights that happen in this life
are accidental to this perfection.*

Background

In this chapter, the author encourages us to continue following the humble movement of love within our hearts. Doing so will help us to find our way through life and bring us to our final destination in heaven. Following this interior movement of love contains the substance of perfection which, in his mind, is nothing other than a good will directed toward God and the sense of fulfillment and joy that flows from it. All perfection, all goodness, all holiness requires having a good will. Everything else is accidental (or secondary). All other joys and consolations, whether they are sensible or spiritual, depend on this one underlying cause. In this life, these accidental (or secondary) elements of perfection can be absent or present without affecting the state of our souls and thus our relationship with God. Perfection on earth consists simply in possessing a good will—and nothing else. During our lives on earth, we may experience long periods of aridity and desolation without them ever affecting the nature of our relationship with God. In heaven, however, these accidental (or secondary) elements will be united to our wills without any separation, similar to the way the body is united to the soul. Those of us who have experienced this close union of wills with God during our earthly lives are willing (even happy) to go without these sensible and spiritual consolations, since we experience their loss as somehow being in accordance with his providential plan for us.

SO I beg you, tend eagerly toward this humble movement of love in your heart and follow it. It will be your guide in this life and bring you to the bliss of heaven in the next. It is the substance of all good living, and without it no good work may be begun or ended. It is nothing other than a good will in harmony with God, and the sort of pleasure and gladness you experience in your will at all He does.

Such a good will is the substance of all perfection. All delight and comforts, both physical and spiritual, however holy they may be, are superfluous accidents in comparison. I call them "accidents," because they may or may not be present without affecting its essence. I am thinking of this life, of course, since in the happiness of heaven they will be united inseparably with their substance, as the body is with the soul. Their substance here on earth is the good, spiritual will. I am sure that whoever experiences this perfect will, as far as it is possible in this life, would be as happy and glad not to have such consolations and delights as to have them, if such is the will of God.

Entering the Cloud

- *Do you agree that holiness has to do primarily with uniting our wills with God's? Do you agree that everything else— even sensible and spiritual consolations—is secondary?*

- *Do you agree that there is a difference between earthly and heavenly perfection? How does the author describe this difference? How would you describe it?*

- *How do we know if our wills are at one with God's? How do we know when they are not?*

- *What are some of the accidental or secondary elements of holiness? Which of these do you consider the most important? Which do you consider the least important? Which would you be able to do without? Which would you joyfully be able to do without?*

Chapter Fifty

*What is chaste love; why sensible comforts come very seldom
to some creatures and very often to others.*

Background

In this chapter, the author encourages us to continue cultivating
the meek and humble movement of love within our hearts. As
contemplatives, we must find our true joy in doing God's will and
consider all other joys and consolations as secondary. We must
welcome such gifts when they come and not be upset with their
absence. The author warns us not to become overly dependent on
these lesser goods, as if we loved God for their sake rather than
his own. One sign we are succumbing to this danger is when we
start complaining about the absence of these secondary goods in
our lives. Rather than trusting the Lord and resigning ourselves to
his will, we start complaining about the discomfort their absence
brings into our lives. The author points out that people have different dispositions and that God takes them into account when
distributing these secondary goods. He goes on to say that God will
console those with delicate spiritual dispositions to help them put
up with the various trials and temptations encountered in this life.
God will also help those with weak bodily dispositions by giving
tears and other consolations to purify their souls when they are too
weak to do penance for their sins. Still others, who are relatively
strong in body and soul, will rarely need any secondary joys and
consolations during their earthly sojourn.

The author does not wish to make a judgment about which
of these kinds of individuals is holiest in the eyes of the Lord. He
believes that only God knows the true state of a person's soul and
asks us not to get involved in such a serious judgment.

TEXT

THUS you can see we should direct all our attention to this lowly movement of love in our will. We should be indifferent toward all other comforts and delights, whether physical or spiritual, however pleasant or holy, courteous or seemly. If they come, welcome them, but do not depend too much on them for fear of becoming weak. It drains too much out of you to stay long in such pleasant feelings and tears. You may even be moved to love God for the sake of having them. You will know this is so by seeing if you overly complain when they are gone. If this be so, your love is not yet chaste and perfect. For a love that is chaste and perfect, though it allows that the body is fed and comforted by such delightful feelings and tears, does not grumble when they are lacking but is pleased not to have them, if it be God's will. And yet in some contemplation is often accompanied by comforts of this kind, while others have them but seldom.

All this depends on the disposition and will of God and is according to the need or good of each person. For some are so weak and so tender in spirit that unless they were comforted by feeling such delight, they would not be able to bear the diversity of temptations and tribulations that they suffer and struggle with in this life from their physical and spiritual enemies. And there are some who are so weak in their bodily constitution that they cannot perform difficult penances for their cleansing. Our Lord graciously cleanses such folk in spirit by such sweet tears and emotions. On the other hand, there are those who are so strong spiritually that they can receive sufficient comfort from their souls—in offering up of this reverent, humble movement of love and obedience of will—that they do not need to be fed with such sweet emotions. Only God knows which of these is holier or dearer to Him. I certainly do not.

Entering the Cloud

- *Do you agree that holiness consists in uniting your will with God's and that all else is secondary?*

- *How would you go about identifying the secondary goods in your life? Through prayer, spiritual reading, spiritual direction? How do you know when you are treating these secondary goods appropriately? How do you know when you are putting them before God?*

- *What kind of complaining do you do when things important to you are absent from your life?*

- *Do you experience these secondary joys and consolations frequently? From time to time? Hardly ever?*

- *Does their frequency (or lack thereof) have anything to do with your physical, mental, or spiritual makeup? Do you agree that we should not use them to gauge the level of our spiritual maturity? Do you agree that God alone can make such a judgment?*

Chapter Fifty-one

We should be careful not to understand in a physical way
what is meant in a spiritual way, especially when
understanding the words "in" and "up."

Background

In this chapter, the author reminds us that there is a literal and a spiritual way of interpreting reality. The word "heart," for example, can refer to the physical organ itself or to the rational appetite of the soul, called the "will." He asks us to take great care in keeping these interpretive approaches to reality distinct, especially since there is great danger when a spiritual reality is given a material interpretation. Words such as "in" and "up," for example, can mean one thing in the spiritual realm and something entirely different in the material. Upon hearing or reading about the cloud of unknowing, a recent convert to the faith may go against the counsel of his or her spiritual director and attempt to implement instructions intended for someone much further along the way of discipleship. As a result, intellectual pride can take the place of humility and we can end up mistakenly convincing ourselves that we are called to leapfrog the ascetical life and go straight into the mystical. We end up thinking we are performing deep spiritual exercises when, in reality, we have fallen prey to the plan of the evil one and are walking down a path swiftly leading to the death of both body and soul. Giving a spiritual reality a material interpretation can thus turn us away from the path of wisdom to that of madness. This chapter reminds us not to mistake the spiritual for the material and cautions those who are beginners in the spiritual life against taking their spiritual well-being into their own hands.

TEXT

THEREFORE, attend humbly to this blind movement of love in your heart. I do not mean in your physical heart but in your spiritual heart, that is, your will. Be careful not to understand "physical" when "spiritual" is intended. For the physical and earthly fantasies of those with a curious and imaginative mind lead to great error.

You can see an example of this when I tell you to hide your desire for God from Him as best you can. If, for example, I had told you to show your desire to God, you would have understood it in a much more physical sense than you do now, when I tell you to hide it. For you now know that what is deliberately hidden is cast into the depths of your soul. So I think it is important to be very careful in understanding words spoken with a spiritual intent so that you will understand them not physically but spiritually, as they are meant. I think it is especially important to be wary of the words "in" and "up." The misunderstanding of these two words has caused much error and wrongdoing in those wishing to be contemplatives. I know something of this from experience, and something from hearsay, and of these errors I now intend to say something.

A young disciple in God's school, newly converted, thinks that, because of the brief time he has given to penance and prayer—performed as a result of counsel from his confessor—he can engage in contemplation, about which he has heard people speak or read, or perhaps has even read himself. When people like this hear of the work of contemplation—and especially the phrase, "how a man shall draw all his knowledge within himself," or how "he shall climb above himself"—they immediately misunderstand these words. They do so because of their spiritual blindness and the earthiness and curiosity of their natural wit and think that, because they find in themselves a natural desire to hide things, they are called to contemplation by grace. So that, if their director does not agree that they should begin contemplating, they grumble against his counsel and think—and perhaps say to others who are like-minded—that they can find no one who truly understands them. And so, out of the boldness and presumption of their curious wit, they leave humble prayer and penance too soon and begin what they think is really spiritual for their soul. And this work, if it is truly understood, is neither physical nor spiritual. In short, it is against nature, and the devil is its chief proponent. It is the fastest way to kill both body and soul, for it is madness and not wisdom, and it makes a man insane. But they do not think so, since they seek in this work to think of nothing but God.

Entering the Cloud

- *Do you agree that there is both a material and a spiritual way of interpreting reality? Do you think there may be a danger in taking either way to the extreme?*

- *Do you think it may be dangerous to interpret a material reality in a spiritual sense—and vice versa?*

- *Do you agree that the will is the spiritual heart of the human person? If so, in what sense? How far would you be willing to extend such an interpretation? Are there any dangers in such an interpretation?*

- *What do the words "in" and "up" mean to the author when taken in the spiritual sense? What happens when a spiritual interpretation is transferred back to the material plane? What possible mistakes might a beginner in the spiritual life make upon hearing the phrase, "Lift up your hearts?" How would someone more spiritually mature interpret it?*

Chapter Fifty-two

How these young presumptuous disciples misunderstand the word "in" and the deceits that follow from it.

Background

In this chapter, the author tells us about the mistakes beginners can make when trying to learn the exercise involved in penetrating the cloud of unknowing. Although beginners like ourselves have heard of the importance of putting our outward senses aside and allowing our inward senses to work within us, we fail to understand precisely what this means. Rather than setting our five senses aside and readying ourselves internally for the spiritual quest ahead, we hastily decide to turn our outward senses in upon ourselves. This use of our physical senses for something they were not originally intended overextends the imagination and creates the potential for great physical, mental, and spiritual strain. The result is that we end up reversing the order of nature by turning our brains in upon themselves and allowing the evil one, the "angel of light" and "master of disguises," to create an illusion of God's quiet presence in our hearts, one seemingly free of all temptation and sinful thoughts. The evil one is eager to keep this illusion alive, since he does not wish to get in the way of his own work, nor does he want us to suspect him to be quietly at work behind the scenes.

TEXT

THE madness I speak of is caused in this way. They read and hear it said that they should stop the external working of their mind and work interiorly. And because they do not know what this inward work is, they do it wrong. For they turn their actual physical minds inward toward their bodies, which is against nature, and strain as if to see spiritually with their physical eyes and to hear within with their physical ears and so forth with smelling, tasting, and so on inwardly in the same way. In doing so, they pervert the course of nature and strain their imagination so much that they eventually turn their brain in their heads. And at once the devil deceives them with some false lights or sounds, sweet smells in their noses, wonderful tastes in their mouths, and glowing heat and burning in their breasts, guts, backs, loins, or limbs.

In all this fantasy, they think they are peacefully contemplating God, unimpeded by vain thoughts. And so they are in a manner of speaking, for they are so full of falsehood that a little vanity does not bother them. And why? Because the same fiend is working on them now who would be tempting them were they on the right path. He is the chief proponent of this work. You know very well that he would not get them in his usual way. However, he does not take all thought of God from them, lest they become suspicious.

Entering the Cloud

- *The internal senses are usually identified as reason, will, memory, imagination, and common sense. Why are they called internal senses?*

- *Do you think the analogy with the external senses holds? How are these internal senses distinguished from the external senses? Must there be five? Does the author follow this breakdown? If so, then why does he identify the will with the heart in an earlier chapter?*

- *Why does he say it is dangerous to turn the five bodily senses inward? Do you agree with him? Do you agree with him that this inward turn of the bodily senses is the work of the evil one? How else could it be explained?*

Chapter Fifty-three

The various unseemly practices that follow those who lack experience in this work of contemplation.

Background

In this chapter, the author points out some of the shocking and unseemly conduct of those who think they are experienced in walking the way of unknowing but are in fact under the influence of the evil one. Some look like diseased sheep; others seem to have worms in their heads; still others pipe as if they have no breath; while others make a variety of unseemly sounds. The author says that some of these poor souls may be able to maintain control of themselves while in public but resort to such behavior once they are in their own homes. They act in this way while remaining thoroughly convinced they are doing everything for the love of God and in order to uphold the divine truth. The author believes they have succumbed to the wiles of the evil one and will go mad unless God takes pity on them. He does not mean to say that all the servants of the evil one display all of these strange characteristics (although this is not beyond the realm of possibility). He is merely pointing out that all hypocrites and heretics will display this unseemly behavior to some degree. He warns us to be careful around people who hang their heads, stare with their mouths open, cannot seem to sit still, or speak while poking their fingers in their chests, stamping their feet on the ground, or laughing at a person's every word.

The author does not mean to imply that all of these actions are wrong in themselves or even that the persons performing them are grave sinners. He is merely saying it is a sign of pride, eccentric behavior, and an unruly desire for knowledge. He also points out that such restlessness of mind and instability of heart point to a thorough lack of knowledge of the exercises he is trying to promote. He points out the complete incongruity of the body taking control of a person in such a way and identifies such a vast array of these disturbing behaviors so that those seeking to implement his teaching may have something by which to measure themselves.

Text

THOSE deceived in this false work (or in something similar) exhibit extraordinary behavior far beyond those of God's true disciples, who are always proper in their physical and spiritual conduct. But it is not so for these others! Whoever looks upon them where they sit will see them staring with their eyes open as if they were mad and acting as if they saw the devil. It is good for them to be wary, for the devil is not far away. Some of them squint as though they were dumb sheep beaten severely on the head and about to die. Some hang their heads on one side as if a worm were in their ears. Some pipe when they should speak, as if there were no spirit in their bodies—the proper condition of a hypocrite. Some cry and whine because they are in such a hurry to say what they think. Heretics are like this, and all who with presumptuous and curious minds will always maintain error.

Someone seeing everything they do would witness many unruly and unseemly practices flowing from this error. Nevertheless, there are some who are so clever that they can restrain themselves in the presence of others. But if they could be seen at home, they would not be able to hide. I also think that, whoever directly contradicts their opinion would soon see them burst out at some point—and yet they think that all they do is for the love of God and to maintain the truth. I truly believe that, unless God works a miracle to make them stop, they will "love God" in this way until they go mad all the way to the devil. I am not saying that the devil has so perfect a servant that he is deceived and infected with all the fantasies I describe here. I do say, however, that though he may not entirely possess any hypocrite or heretic here on earth, he is responsible for some I have mentioned, or will mention, if God permits.

For some men are so prone to these curious tricks of deportment that, when they should be listening, they twist their heads quaintly on one side and stick their chins up. They gape with their mouths as if they hear with their mouths and not with their ears. When some speak, they use their fingers for emphasis, either on their fingers or on their breasts, or on the person they are speaking to. Some cannot sit still, stand still, or lie still unless they are either wagging their feet or doing something with their hands. Some row with their arms when speaking, as if they need to swim a great distance. Some smile and laugh at every other word they speak, as if they were giggling girls and nice jugglers who did not know how to behave. It would be much better to be modest in one's behavior with sober bodily bearing of and mirth in one's manner.

I am not saying that all these unseemly practices are great sins in themselves or that all who do them are great sinners. I do say, however, that if these unseemly and unruly practices govern a person so that he cannot leave them at will, then they are tokens of pride, curious wit, unruly behavior, and covetous knowledge. To be even more precise, they are signs of an unstable heart, a restless mind, and a lack of capacity to follow the practices of this book. This is the only reason why I set out so many of these errors here, so that a contemplative can test his progress by them.

Entering the Cloud

- *To what extent are the people described in this chapter displaying signs of mental illness?*

- *Are mystics and deeply spiritual people sometimes mistaken for mentally deranged people? What has been your experience, if any?*

- *Why does the author insist that the mind governs the body— and not vice versa? Is it possible for the animal side to overwhelm the spiritual side of us? Is it possible to become so confused that we mistake bodily senses for spiritual senses?*

- *Is the author against these unseemly forms of actions in themselves or simply when they are used as a way of determining the authenticity of a call?*

- *What would you consider to be inappropriate behavior for today's disciple?*

- *What characteristics must someone called to the contemplative way display today?*

- *Do you agree that following the lead of the evil one will ultimately drive you out of your mind?*

Chapter Fifty-four

Through the work of contemplation, a man governs himself wisely and becomes seemly in both body and soul.

Background

In this chapter, the author tells us that the exercise of penetrating the cloud of unknowing as he describes it will make us sound in both mind and body. Even those who are not naturally attractive will be made so by the practice, and all people will be grateful to be in our presence. He encourages us to see the grace of this form of prayer, telling us that it will help us to govern ourselves and to discern the proper path at all times. We would also know how to make ourselves all things to everyone who lives with us, regardless of where they are on their spiritual journey. People would marvel at our wisdom and at how it radiates truth and sincerity without any hint of pretense or hypocrisy. Such brilliance, he tells us, comes not from ourselves but from God and is very different from what comes out of those who spend all their time polishing their words and phrases and practicing their tones and gestures in order to make themselves appear holy before others. The truly humble person communicates with words and gestures that flow straight from the heart. If they are true, such words will be spoken truthfully and resonate in a way that will pierce the heart of the listeners. Falsehood, on the other hand, is revealed in its false ring and can be detected even in those who have normal-sounding voices.

TEXT

ALL who take up this work of contemplation discover that it has a positive effect on the body as well as on the soul, for it makes them attractive in the eyes of all who see them. So much so that the ugliest man or woman alive who becomes a contemplative by the grace of God finds that he is suddenly different. He is changed by

184

grace, and each good man he sees is glad to be with him, spiritually refreshed and drawn to God by his presence.

So seek this gift of grace, for whoever really has it will be able to govern himself and all that belongs to him by virtue of it. It gives him discretion, when he needs it, to understand the needs and dispositions of others. It helps him to understand everyone he talks to, habitual sinner or not, without sinning himself. He does this to the surprise of those who see him, drawing them by grace to the very work of contemplation that he follows.

His face and words are full of spiritual wisdom, fire, and sober truthfulness without any falsehood, and he is far from the affected pretensions of the hypocrites. For some people focus all their attention on learning how to speak eloquently and to avoid making fools of themselves by using many piping words and devout gestures. They are more anxious to appear holy in the sight of men than to be so in the sight of God and His angels. These folks will worry and grieve more over unorthodox ritual or an inappropriate word or gesture than they will for a thousand vain thoughts and sinful impulses, which they have deliberately gathered into themselves or recklessly indulged in the sight of God and the saints and angels in heaven. Ah, Lord God! Where there is so much pride within, there are so many plentiful, humble words without. I am ready to grant that it is fitting and seemly that those who are truly humble inside express the humility of their heart with words and gestures externally. But I cannot say they should be expressed in broken or in piping voices against the plain disposition of the nature of the speaker. If they are genuine, they should speak with sincerity, and the speaker's voice should be as sound as his spirit. If a man who has a naturally loud and powerful voice speaks in a pathetic and high-pitched voice (assuming he is not ill or is not talking with God or his confessor), then it is a clear sign of hypocrisy in young and old alike.

What more shall I say of these venomous deceits? Unless they have the grace to leave off such piping hypocrisy, I truly believe that, between the secret pride in their inmost hearts and the humble words on their lips, their foolish souls will easily sink into sorrow.

Entering the Cloud

- *Do you agree that the exercise involved in penetrating the cloud of unknowing can help in making us sound in both body and soul?*

- *What are some of the presuppositions about the relation of body and soul behind such a statement?*

- *What are some of the dangers such a presupposition might bring along with it?*

- *Is there any way of maintaining a sound body-and-soul connection while steering clear of judging a person's spiritual maturity according to his or her outward appearances? How does the author deal with this possibility?*

- *According to the author, is it possible to be spiritually mature yet also physically grotesque? Have you ever met someone who was beautiful on the inside and "plain" on the outside?*

- *What is the key truth in this chapter? Does it need to be balanced by any others?*

Chapter Fifty-five

It is wrong for a person with excessive fervor to condemn without discretion.

Background

In this chapter, the author tells us how the evil one often lures us into doing his will. Rather than tempting us with thoughts and actions that are obviously evil, he inflames in us a deep desire to maintain God's law and to stamp out sin in others. We end up busying ourselves with the affairs of other people's lives, much like the bishop of a diocese or the abbot of a monastery. Because this is not our calling, however, we end up becoming so inflamed with externals that we lose sight of the reality of God's love. Although we may say we are moved by the zeal of divine love, our imaginations are actually full of fire and brimstone. The servant is like his master. The evil one, the author explains, is a pure spirit who, when assuming material shape, always reveals the true nature of his mission through some physical characteristic. From his familiarity with the art of necromancy, the author tells us that the devil always has one large and broad nostril that reveals the fires of hell as his true purpose. In a similar way, the evil one inflames the "spiritual nostril" (or imagination) of those who do his bidding so that they blame others immediately for their faults without any deliberation or forethought. They have lost all powers of discretion and are no longer able to distinguish "good from evil, evil from worse, or good from better."

TEXT

THE fiend will deceive some in this way. He will enflame their brains in a remarkable way to keep God's law and destroy sin in all other men. He will never tempt them with anything that is obviously evil. He makes them like busy prelates watching over the various states of Christian living, or as an abbot over his monks. They do not hesitate to reprove others for their faults, as if they had care for their souls. Yet they think they do nothing for God, except telling others their faults. They say they are moved to do so by the fire of charity and because of God's love in their hearts. But they lie. It is the fire of hell that wells up in their minds and imaginations that causes it.

The truth of this comes from what follows. The devil is a spirit, and of his own nature he has no more a body than an angel. Yet when he or an angel assumes a body (with God's permission) to do something to a human being, he still retains some likeness to his natural self. We have an example of this in Holy Writ. Whenever an angel was sent in bodily form in the Old or New Testament, his essential purpose or message was always revealed, either by his name or by some instrument or quality of his appearance. It is the same with the devil. When he appears in bodily form, he manifests in some physical way what his servants are in spirit. An example of this can be seen in the disciples of necromancy, who claim to know how to call up wicked spirits and to whom the fiend has appeared in physical form. In whatever bodily likeness the fiend appears, he always has but one nostril, which is great and wide, and he will gladly turn it up so a man might look into his brain. And his brain contains nothing else than the fire of hell, for the fiend cannot have any other kind of brain. And if he can make a man look, he wants nothing more. For when he looks, he goes mad forever. But a perfect apprentice of necromancy knows this all too well and can so order things that he escapes harm.

So it is as I say, and have said, that whenever the devil takes bodily form, he reveals in some quality of his body what his servants are in spirit. For he so enflames the imagination of his contemplatives with the fire of hell that suddenly, without discretion, they shoot out their curious conceits without any hesitation and will take it upon themselves to blame other men's faults too soon. They do this because they have but one spiritual nostril. For the division in a man's actual nose, which separates one nostril from the other, suggests that a man should have spiritual insight that can distinguish the good from the evil, evil from worse, and good from better, before he passes judgment on anything he has heard or seen done around him. A man's brain spiritually stands for the imagination, for through its nature it dwells and works in the head.

Entering the Cloud

- *Do you believe that the evil one can trick you into thinking you are doing good when, in reality, you are doing evil?*
- *Have you ever met people who love to point out the faults of others but cannot see the evil in their own hearts?*
- *Have you ever felt that way yourself? If so, how did you deal with it?*
- *Have you ever felt as though your imagination were out of your control, as if it were leading you by a chain to places you would rather not go? To what extent is it your own fault? To what extent is it the work of the evil one? To what extent is it a mixture of both?*
- *Is it possible that you sometimes blame the evil one for what are your own shortcomings? Is it possible that you do not pay enough heed to the workings of the evil one in your life?*
- *To what extent has your capacity to distinguish good from evil, evil from worse, and good from better been compromised?*

Chapter Fifty-six

It is wrong to pay more attention to intellectual ability and to those learned in the school of men than to the doctrine and counsel of Holy Church?

Background

In this chapter, the author warns us not to abandon the ordinary teaching and counsel of the Church in favor of speculative academic learning fueled by pride and curiosity. Those of us without a firm grounding in this simple contemplative experience and in the humble life of virtue can easily fall prey to false experiences produced by the evil one. Through such experiences, we believe we have gained access to a purer, more certain knowledge and end up breaking with the saints, sacraments, laws, and ordinances of the Church. We then dilute the demands of the Gospel and attract worldly followers looking for an easier way to heaven. The author insists that those who do not wish to follow the narrow way to heaven will succumb to the soft and easy way to hell. He asks us to examine ourselves to see if we have fallen prey to such pride and confidence in our own intellectual powers. He wishes that all heretics and their followers could see themselves for what they truly are: disciples of the anti-Christ heavily laden with sin and the burdens of the flesh.

TEXT

ALTHOUGH they do not fall into the error I have just described, there are some who, because of their pride, erudition, and natural intellectual curiosity, leave the common doctrine and counsel of Holy Church. Along with all their supporters, they depend too much on their own learning. And because they were never grounded in this humble "blind" experience and in virtuous living, they

190

deserve to have a false experience, feigned and wrought by their spiritual enemy so that they eventually burst out and blaspheme all the saints, sacraments, statutes, and ordinances of Holy Church. Worldly men who think the statutes of Holy Church are too hard to help them amend their lives look to these heretics too soon and readily and support them wholeheartedly because they think they will lead them by a more comfortable way than that ordained by Holy Church.

Now I truly believe that those who refuse to follow the difficult path to heaven will go the soft way to hell. Each man will discover this for himself. I believe that if we could see for ourselves the state of these heretics and their supporters as they will appear on the Last Day, we would see them bowed down not only with the burden of their open presumption in embracing error but also with the horrible sins they have committed secretly in the flesh. For it is said of them that for all their false justice, they are filthy and debauched lechers in secret and rightly called disciples of the Antichrist.

Entering the Cloud

- *Do you agree that intellectual curiosity and pride can get in the way of your spiritual well-being?*

- *How do you know when reason is used in the service of the faith and when it is being used to undermine the faith?*

- *Have you ever met people who are so intellectually full of themselves that they look down upon the opinions of others and even those of the Church?*

- *What is the connection between intellectual pride and religious belief? What is the connection between intellectual pride and heresy?*

- *Is it possible for even devout disciples of Christ to be over-confident in their intellectual powers? What precautions can you take to avoid such pitfalls?*

Chapter Fifty-seven

How these young, presumptuous disciples misunderstand
the word "up" and the deceits that follow from it.

Background

In this chapter, the author emphasizes the spiritual rather than physical nature of the form of contemplative prayer he is promoting. A word like "up" or a phrase like "lift up your hearts" should not be interpreted literally but spiritually. Upon hearing such terms, we should not strain our hearts in order to move them physically to a higher place, but we should look beyond the present limitations of time and space and see that God is calling us to a higher dimension of existence, one that cannot be measured. If we mistake the spiritual for the physical in this way, we will draw all sorts of wrong conclusions and never reap the fruits of true contemplation.

Limiting ourselves to this physical world, we will turn God into an image of our own fanciful whims and give the angels under him vestments and instruments never before imagined. The evil one will contribute to these wild imaginings with delusory sensory experiences that will keep us within the dimensions of our present experience. We will adopt false, eccentric exercises that will do nothing but fan our vanity and steer us away from true devotion. We will think we are like St. Martin, who looked up to heaven when he received a special revelation from God, or St. Stephen, when he lifted his eyes heavenly at the moment of his death, or the Lord himself, who ascended into heaven before his disciples.

The author has nothing against sincere prayerful bodily gestures, but he does not want us to mistake the spiritual realm for the physical, the heavenly for the earthly. We will never penetrate the cloud of unknowing if we limit God and his heavenly court to the present dimension of time and space. To do so would result in our misunderstanding the true nature of God's kingdom and border on idolatry.

TEXT

BUT no more of this at present. It is time to move on and see how these young, presumptuous spiritual disciples misunderstand this other word, "up."

For if they read or hear it read or spoken that men should lift up their hearts to God, they immediately start staring at the stars, as if they wanted to travel beyond the moon and listen for an angel to sing out from heaven. In their imagination, they pierce the planets and make a hole in the firmament to look through. They shape God to their liking, give Him rich clothes, and set Him on a throne, and it is all very strange, much more than any image we have of Him. They depict angels in human shape and set them about each with a different musical instrument in a way much stranger than has ever been heard or seen on earth.

The devil will deceive some of these men quite incredibly. For he sends a sort of dew (they think it is angels' food) coming out of the air and falling softly and pleasantly into their mouths! They have a habit of sitting and gaping as if they were catching flies. Now all this is nothing but deceit, even if it appears holy, for their souls all during this time are empty of real devotion. They have much vanity and falsehood in their hearts, which is caused by their curious practices. So much so that often the devil brings faint sounds in their ears, quaint lights and shining to their eyes, wonderful smells to their noses—and all is false. Still, they do not think so, for they think they have an example of St. Martin, who saw by revelation God wearing His mantle among His angels, and of St. Stephen, who saw our Lord standing in heaven, and of many others, and of Christ Himself, whom His disciples saw ascending bodily to heaven. Therefore, they say we should turn out eyes upward. I readily grant that in our bodily observance we should lift up our eyes and our hands, if the spirit so moves. I am saying, however, that the work of our spirit does not go up or down, from one side to the other, forward or backward, like some physical thing. And why? Because our work is spiritual, not physical, and it is not achieved in a physical manner.

Entering the Cloud

- *Why is it wrong to interpret a spiritual teaching in a literal, physical way?*

- *What does limiting God to the dimensions of space and time say about our understanding of God? What does it say about the way we relate to God? How can such a materialistic interpretation demean God and perhaps even border on idolatry?*

- *How does the Church's sacramental system, which uses material things as a means of entering into relationship with God, escape these pitfalls?*

- *Are the dangers the author raises problematic for all Christians or only for beginners?*

- *Have you ever found yourself interpreting a profound spiritual teaching in an immature way? What safeguards can be put in place to help people avoid making such mistakes?*

Chapter Fifty-eight

We should not consider St. Martin and St. Stephen to be examples of straining our sensible imagination upward during the time of prayer.

Background

In this chapter, the author explains why we should not use the special visions granted to St. Martin and St. Stephen as support for excessively exerting our imaginations and physical senses while at prayer. He points out that both these saints were given these miraculous visions in order to verify profound spiritual truths: for St. Martin, who saw Christ in a person to whom he had given half his cloak, it was to reaffirm God's presence in those in need; for St. Stephen, who saw the heavens open up as he was about to be stoned, it was to strengthen him at the moment of death. These visions conveyed specific spiritual meanings and were not meant to be taken literally. When interpreting them, therefore, we are to remove the hard rind from the soft, sweet-tasting interior and digest the spiritual nourishment within. We should not cheapen them by interpreting them on a purely physical level. The author goes so far as to say that these spiritual insights were given bodily manifestations simply because we would not have been capable of understanding them otherwise. To focus exclusively on the external dimension of these visions, he maintains, does an injustice to both the revealer and the revealed. These visions have very little (if anything) do with how we should physically and sensibly conduct ourselves when at prayer and everything to do with God's loving and quiet presence to us in time of need.

TEXT

AS to what they say about St. Martin and St. Stephen, although they saw such things with their physical eyes, it was clearly a miracle pointing to a spiritual truth. For they know full well that St. Martin's mantle never really covered Christ's body to keep Him warm but was donned miraculously as a sign to all of us who can be saved and who are spiritually united to the body of Christ. Whoever clothes a poor man, and who does any other good physical or spiritual deed for the love of God, does so spiritually to Christ, and they shall be rewarded as if they had done it to Christ's own body. He says this Himself in the Gospel. Yet He thought it not enough, until He affirmed it afterward by a miracle, and so He showed Himself to St. Martin in a special revelation. All visions seen in physical form have spiritual meanings. And I think that, if those who saw them had been sufficiently spiritual, they would never have been shown these physical visions in the first place. Therefore, let us strip off the rough bark and eat the sweet-tasting kernel.

But how? Not as these heretics do, for they are like madmen whose custom it is when they have drunk from some beautiful cup to throw it at the wall and break it. We should not do this sort of thing if we wish to make progress. We who feed on its fruit are not going to despise the tree, nor when we drink break the cup we have drunk from. I would call the tree and the cup the visible miracle and all outward observances that help and do not hinder the work of the spirit. I would call the fruit and the drink the spiritual meaning behind these visible miracles, these outward observances, such as the lifting up of our eyes and our hands to heaven. If they are done at the bidding of the Spirit, they are good; otherwise it is hypocrisy and they are false. If they are true and contain spiritual fruit, why despise them? For men will kiss the cup that holds the wine.

When ascending to heaven, does it really matter if our Lord was actually seen by His mother and His disciples going up into the clouds? When we contemplate, are we to stare upward, looking to see Him standing or sitting in heaven as St. Stephen did? Surely not. He did not reveal Himself in bodily form to St. Stephen to tell us to look physically up to heaven when contemplating, as if we could see Him as St. Stephen did standing, sitting, or lying down. For no one knows whether He is standing, sitting, or lying down in heaven. We do not need to know anything more than that His body is one with His soul. His body and soul, that is, His humanity, is in turn inseparably united with His Godhead. We do not need to know about His sitting, standing, or lying, but that He is there doing what He likes, and that He is, in His body, whatever is best for Him to be. If He shows Himself in any of these postures in a vision to anyone, it is done for some spiritual purpose, not because He is actually adopting that posture in heaven.

Here's an example. The word "standing" signifies a willingness to help. Thus it is commonly said by one friend to another when he is engaged in physical combat: "Bear up, my friend, fight hard, and do not give up too easily, for I shall stand by you." He means not only physical standing, for perhaps this battle is on horse, not on foot, and perhaps it involves charging, not standing. When he says that he will stand by him, he means that he will be ready to help him. This is why our Lord showed Himself physically from heaven to St. Stephen in his martyrdom. He did so not to bid us to look up to heaven but to tell Him and all who suffer persecution for His sake: "I open the firmament of heaven and let you see me standing physically so you may trust that I am standing by you spiritually and am ready to help you by the power of my Godhead. Therefore, stand firm in the faith and suffer bravely the buffeting of those hard stones. For I shall crown you in heaven as your reward, and not only you, but all who suffer persecution for me in any manner." So you can see that these bodily visions were for spiritual purposes.

Entering the Cloud

- *Do you agree that something spiritual often lies beneath the physical?*

- *Do you agree that concrete events can carry such spiritual meanings with them? Have you ever experienced such an event? To what extent can such an event be considered miraculous? To what extent can the spiritual meaning it conveys be considered a message from God?*

- *How often have you missed such messages? What can you do to become more adept at sensing them? What guidelines should you follow?*

- *Can such revelations go against the teachings of the Church? Can they go against the basic tenets of the spiritual life?*

- *What is wrong with interpreting the visions of St. Martin and St. Stephen in an overly literal way?*

Chapter Fifty-nine

*When at prayer, we should not take the bodily ascension of Christ
as an example for straining our sensible imagination upward.
Time, place, and the body should all be forgotten
in this spiritual work.*

Background

In this chapter, the author tells us not to use Christ's bodily ascension into heaven as evidence of our need to strain our bodies and imaginations upward during times of prayer. Intimately related to the mystery of our redemption, Christ's ascension was a unique occurrence in the history of humanity. While it is true that it took place bodily and spiritually, it is also true that Jesus first had to die, rise, and be glorified before he could ascend to the Father. Since this bodily transfiguration awaits us only on the Last Day, it would be a mistake for us to look to Christ's ascension for evidence on how we should conduct ourselves at prayer during our earthly sojourn. Christ's ascension, in other words, involved his glorified, resurrected body and should not be used as an example of how we should pray in our earthly bodies. In our present condition, it is not possible for us to ascend bodily into heaven as Jesus did. In our present state, we can do so only spiritually through the movement of prayer, not literally in the physical, bodily order. For this reason, Christ's ascension tells us nothing about the movement of our bodies and sensible imaginations while at prayer. The author insists, moreover, that when seeking to penetrate the cloud of unknowing, we should put aside all concern for time, place, and the physical world. Christ's ascension points to the transfigured joy we will share with him in the world to come and has nothing to do with straining our bodies and sensible imagination during our lives on earth.

TEXT

IF you point to our Lord's Ascension and say that it must have some physical significance, since it was a physical body that ascended and He was true God and true man, my answer is that He had been dead and was clothed in immortality as we shall be on the day of judgment. At that time, we shall be so subtle in body and soul that we shall be able to go physically wherever we wish as swiftly as we can now go anywhere mentally in thought, whether it be up or down, on one side or on the other, behind or before. It will be all the same to us, and good, as the scholars say. But now you cannot go to heaven physically, but only spiritually. At that time, it will be so spiritual that it will not seem physical at all: neither up nor down, on one side or the other, behind or before.

When you read "lift up" or "go in" or that the work of this book involves a "movement," everyone wishing to live the spiritual life (and especially those who seek to follow the work of this book) clearly understand that this movement does not go up or down and that it is not from one place to another. Although it may sometimes be called "a rest," still they should not think that it is abiding in a place without moving from it. For the perfection of contemplation is so pure and so spiritual in itself that, when properly understood, it would be seen far removed from a movement from any place.

It might be better to call it a sudden "changing" than a "movement from place." For time, place, and body should be forgotten in all spiritual matters. So be careful not to take the physical Ascension of Christ as an example, so that you try to lift your imagination physically upward, as if you were climbing beyond the moon. It cannot be so spiritually! For if you were to ascend bodily into heaven, as Christ did, you could use it as an example. But no one can do that except God, for He says, "No one may ascend to heaven but he who descended from heaven and became man for the love of man." [19] If it were possible (which it is not), it would still be for a fullness of spiritual activity, and solely by the power of the spirit, far removed from any physical stress or strain on our bodily imagination, which would make it go up or in, on one side or on the other. So let go of such falsehood; it cannot be so.

200

Entering the Cloud

- *Do you agree that Christ's ascension was a unique event in the history of humanity? If so, in what ways was it unique? Does it apply to the way we should conduct ourselves during our present earthly sojourn or to our life in the world to come?*

- *Do you agree that Christ's ascension should not be used as evidence for straining our bodies and imaginations upward during times of prayer?*

- *Is this because Christ's ascension involved a glorified, resurrected body, and we are still burdened by our earthly, mortal ones?*

- *Does Christ's ascension tell us anything at all about the nature of Christian prayer?*

- *What errors is the author trying to point out? Do these errors in any way apply to you?*

Chapter Sixty

The high road and the nearest way to heaven come through desires, not through distance.

Background

In this chapter, the author reminds us that heaven cannot be limited to the dimensions of time and space. Even though certain passages of Scripture depict Jesus as ascending into and the Holy Spirit as descending from a physical place (see Acts 1:9 and Mark 1:9–10), we must not overlook the underlying otherworldly character of God's heavenly abode. To collapse heaven into time and space overlooks the fact that these dimensions are themselves a part of God's creation. God does not exist in time but beyond it. The fact that he visited earth in the person of Jesus Christ does not negate the transcendental, other dimensional nature of the Godhead. We get to heaven not by going up or down, as if we could somehow pinpoint God's presence in the here and now. We get there not by crossing a distance at all but through the desire to be there, which is itself a divine gift. Although it may be depicted as such at times, heaven is not exclusively a place but a state of mind. If our hearts are in the right place, we can be in heaven while still on earth. To enter the threshold of the sacred, we need not move our spirits up or down but merely allow the love of God to enter our heart and dwell within us.

TEXT

PERHAPS you are wondering how this could be. You think you have very good evidence that heaven is up, for Christ ascended physically upward and sent the Holy Spirit, as He promised, from above and was seen by all His disciples, and this is our belief. And so you think since you have such evidence, why should you not direct your mind upward when you pray?

My answer, though weak and feeble, is the best I can do. Since Christ ascended physically and then sent the Holy Spirit in visible form, it was more fitting that it was upward and from above than downward and from below, behind or before, on one side or on the other. Except for this appropriateness, He did not need to go upward or downward to find the nearest way to us. For heaven is spiritually as much "down" as it is "up," as much "before" as it is "behind," as much "one side" as it is "the other." So whoever truly desired to be in heaven would be there spiritually in an instant. For the high road and the nearest way there is through desire and not through distance. And so St. Paul said of himself and many others that, although our bodies are presently here on earth, nevertheless we are living in heaven. [20] He meant their love and their desire, which is, spiritually, their life. Surely the soul is as truly where the object of its love is as it is in its body which depends on it and to which it gives life. If we go to heaven spiritually, we need not strain our spirit up or down, or on one side or on the other.

Entering the Cloud

- *Is heaven a place? Is it a state of mind? Is it perhaps a little bit of both?*

- *What are the dangers of limiting heaven to the dimensions of space and time? What are the dangers of limiting it solely to the spiritual?*

- *Is the author denying a material dimension of heaven or merely saying that it cannot be reduced to the dimensions of space and time?*

- *If Christian belief affirms a continuity of our earthly and glorified bodies, must there not be some recognizable material element in the hereafter?*

- *What is the relationship between glorified matter and the realm of spirit?*

Chapter Sixty-one

All bodily things are subject to spiritual things;
the course of nature follows this rule, not the contrary.

Background

In this chapter, the author reminds us that the physical realm is subject to the spiritual—and not vice versa. He uses the Lord's ascension as an example. When the appointed time arrived, Jesus ascended body and soul into heaven. He returned to the Father in the fullness of his divinity and glorified humanity, an inseparable union made possible by the mystery of the Incarnation. This extraordinary return to heavenly glory took place through the power of God's Spirit and not through the power of Jesus' humanity. The author goes on to say that the same principle applies to the practice involved in penetrating the cloud of unknowing. Whenever the soul turns to the Lord in this exercise of prayer, the body follows the work of the spirit. The human body stands upright and is meant to follow the spirit's gaze into the heavens. Because it is the body's role to imitate the spirit, it is wrong to force the spirit to strain after the way of the flesh. God did not make us that way. He wants our superior powers to rule the inferior and not the other way around. Since speech is a bodily function, however, he points out the necessity of using bodily metaphors when speaking about spiritual things. When using words such as "up" or "down," "in" or "out," "behind" or "before," "on one side" or "on the other," we must not interpret them literally but spiritually. To do otherwise would be to turn the message inside out and distort its spiritual intent.

TEXT

STILL it is important to lift up our physical eyes and hands to the heavenly sky. I mean only if we are so moved in the spirit. For all physical things are subject to the spiritual and are ruled by it, not vice versa.

An example of this appears in the Ascension of our Lord. When the appointed time came for Him to return to the Father in His physical humanity, which never was or will be separated from His divinity, through the power of God's Spirit, His humanity followed the one Person. The outward manifestation of this was, most suitably, upward.

This same subjection of the body to the spirit may be seen in those who seek to carry out the spiritual work of this book. For when a soul is determined to perform this work of contemplation, at the same time, and unknown to himself, his body which before he began tended to stoop to one side or the other because it was easier, by virtue of the spirit now sets itself upright, following physically what has been done spiritually. And this is most fitting.

And so it is fitting that man, who is the seemliest creature in body ever made by God, is not made crooked bending earthward, like all the other animals, but upright facing heavenward. And why? So the physical body could reflect the likeness of the spiritual soul, which should be upright spiritually and not crooked. Notice that I say "upright spiritually" and not "physically." For how can a soul, which by nature has no physical aspects, be strained upright physically? It cannot be done.

And so be careful not to understand physically what is meant spiritually, although it is spoken in concrete words, such as "up or down, in or out, behind or before, on one side or on other." For although something may be ever so spiritual in itself, if we are to speak of it at all, we must use physical words, since speech is a physical action of the tongue, which is an instrument of the body. But what of it? Shall it be understood in a physical sense? No, it is to be understood spiritually.

Entering the Cloud

- *Do you agree with the author's insights about the relationship between the spiritual and the physical? Why must the body follow the spiritual—and not vice versa? Does this apply to all things or only to the spiritual life?*

- *In what sense is the spirit or soul superior to the physical body? Can you think of any sense in which is it not? Must physical disease, for example, be considered the result of some hidden spiritual malaise?*

- *Can the author's valid insights sometimes be taken too far?*

- *Have you ever interpreted something spiritual in an overly physical way? Have you ever interpreted something physical in an overly spiritual way?*

- *Is there any other way to speak about spiritual things besides using physical metaphors?*

Chapter Sixty-two

*How we can know when our spiritual work is beneath us
or outside us, when it is with us or within us, and
when it is above us and under our God.*

Background

In this chapter, the author shows us our place in the order of things and tells us how to interpret our actions accordingly. He begins by explaining the spiritual meaning of words that have an underlying material connotation. In this way, he hopes to help us to better discern when a particular spiritual activity is beneath us, within us, or above us. All material things, for example, are outside of us and naturally below us. This holds true even for the sun, the moon, and the stars, which are physically above us. He goes on to say that, regardless of how much holier they are than us because of their virtuous lives and response to God's grace, all angels and saints are equal to us by nature. For this reason, we can aspire to one day be like them.

He goes on to say that our souls themselves have three principal powers or faculties (mind, reason, and will), and two secondary ones (imagination and sensuality). These means are how our souls exert themselves in the world. God alone, he tells us, is above us in the realm of nature. That is to say, he is beyond the physical world in the cloud of unknowing. Finally, he tells us that whenever we come upon the word "yourself" in a spiritual reading, we should take that to mean the "soul" rather than the "body." If we fail to do so, grave and erroneous consequences will follow. The nature and value of our work, moreover, are determined by the powers of our soul and whether they focus on objects that are beneath us, within us, or above us. Through all this, the author is trying to help us understand the nature of our spiritual existence in the world by showing us our place in the universe and the nature and extent of our spiritual powers.

TEXT

SO that you will be better able to know how physical words should be understood spiritually, I will describe for you the spiritual meaning of some words that are often used in the spiritual life. In this way, you will know clearly and without error when your spiritual activity is beneath you and outside of you, and when it is within you and even with you, and when it is above you and under your God.

All physical things are outside of your soul and beneath its nature. Yes, although they are above your body, the sun, the moon, and all the stars are nevertheless beneath your soul.

All angels and souls, although strengthened and adorned with grace and virtue, for which they are above you in purity, are nevertheless on the same level with you in nature.

Your soul has within itself by nature three principal powers: the mind (which includes memory), reason, and will; and two secondary ones: imagination and sensuality.

Only God is above you in nature.

Whenever you find the word "yourself" in books on the spiritual life, understand your soul, not your body. The worth and quality of what you are doing—whether it be beneath you, within you, or above you—is based on what the powers of your soul are working on.

Entering the Cloud

- *Do you agree with the author's basic presentation? Are all material things beneath us? Are we of the same nature as the saints and angels, despite their superiority in holiness? Is God alone above us in nature?*

- *Do you agree that the soul has the primary powers of understanding, reason, and will, as well as the secondary powers of imagination and sensuality?*

- *Do you agree that when coming upon the word "yourself" in a spiritual reading you should read "soul" rather than "body?"*

- *Do you agree with the author's hierarchical rendering of the universe and of the human person?*

- *Do you think people will have an easy or difficult time accepting the author's rendering today?*

Chapter Sixty-three

On the faculties of the soul in general. How the Mind in particular is a principal power, containing in it all the other powers and all their activities.

Background

In this chapter, the author tells us about the various powers of the soul. The mind, he says, contains and comprehends all the other powers: reason, will, imagination, and sensuality. Its only activity is its comprehension of the other powers. Although the soul is not divisible, it has principal powers for spiritual objects and secondary powers for material objects. The mind is a principal power because it comprehends all the other powers as well as the objects upon which these powers work. Reason and will are principal powers because they deal solely with spiritual things. Imagination and sensuality are secondary powers because they work in the body through the bodily senses and deal with material things. The soul, the author reminds us, needs the help of reason and will in order to know the origins of the action and the mode of being of material objects. It cannot do so through imagination and sensuality alone.

TEXT

THE power of the mind, generally speaking, does no work by itself, whereas reason and will do, and so do imagination and sensuality. The mind contains and embraces all these four powers and their works. It works in no other sense but this.

I call some powers of a soul principal and some secondary. Not because a soul is divisible, for it is not, but because all those things upon which they work are divisible, and some are principal, as are all spiritual things, and some secondary and all physical things.

The two principal working powers, Reason and Will, work entirely on spiritual things, without the help of the other two secondary powers. Imagination and sensuality work in all forms of animal and physical things, whether they are present or absent in the body and with the bodily senses. By them alone, without the help of reason and of will, a soul would never come to know the ethical conditions of physical creation or the cause of their being and actions.

This is why reason and will are called principal powers, for they work in a spiritual way without any physical aspect and why imagination and sensuality are secondary, for they work in the body with bodily instruments, which are our five senses. Mind is called a principal faculty, for it contains spiritually in itself not only all the other powers but also all those things through which they work. Let me show you.

Entering the Cloud

- *Do you agree with the author's analysis of the powers of the soul? Are his distinctions clear enough for you? What needs more explanation?*

- *What does he mean by the term "power" of the soul? How are the soul's powers different from the soul itself? Can the soul function without its powers? What is the difference between the principal and secondary powers of the soul?*

- *What is the difference between reason and mind? Is mind a principal power in the same way as are reason and will?*

- *If reason and will deal only with spiritual things, then why are they necessary for helping the soul to know the source of activity and the mode of being of material things?*

- *Do even material things have a certain spiritual dimension to them?*

Chapter Sixty-four

On the other two principal powers, reason and will,
and their activity before and after original sin.

Background

In this chapter, the author discusses the nature of reason and will, especially about how they acted before and after humanity's fall. He reminds us that reason, will, and their objects are contained and comprehended in the mind. As a power of the soul, reason provides us with our moral compass. It enables us to tell the difference between good and evil, bad from worse, good from better, worse from worst, and better from best. Before the Fall, it could do this naturally, unassisted by the influence of divine grace. After the Fall, however, it can do so only with the assistance of divine grace. The will, by way of contrast, is the power of the soul that enables us to actually choose the good designated by reason. Through the will, we are able to love, desire, and rest in God with our whole hearts and with our full consent. Before the Fall, the will was able to value everything for its true worth and therefore could not make a mistake in choosing what to love or what to do. After the Fall, however, it could do so only with the help of divine grace. Because of the effects of original sin, it sometimes accepts as good what is really evil and only has the appearance of good. Reason and will are the two principal powers of the soul. They, along with their objects, are contained and comprehended in the mind, the intellectual or rational part of the human soul.

TEXT

REASON is the power by which we tell the difference between evil from good, bad from worse, good from better, worse from worst, better from best. Before man sinned, reason could do all this by nature. But now reason is so blinded by original sin that it cannot do so unless it is enlightened by grace. Both reason itself and the means by which it works are included and contained in the mind.

Will is the power by which we choose good, after it has been determined by reason, and the power by which we love good and desire good, and eventually with complete satisfaction and consent rest fully in God. Before man sinned, his will could not be wrong in its choosing, its living, or in any of its actions because it was able by nature to appreciate each thing as it was. But it cannot do so now, unless it is anointed with grace. For often because of the infection of original sin, will takes a thing for good that is completely evil and has only the appearance of good. Both the will and what it wills are contained and embraced by the mind.

Entering the Cloud

- *Would it be accurate to say that reason and will are the rational powers of the soul? If so how do they relate to the secondary, nonrational powers (imagination and sensuality)? How do they themselves interrelate? Do they operate dependently or independently of each other?*

- *Is the will naturally drawn toward the good in itself or only the good as presented to it by reason?*

- *How were both reason and will influenced by the Fall? After the Fall, was reason's capacity to distinguish good from evil completely destroyed or merely impeded? Was the will's capacity to choose the good completely destroyed or merely impeded?*

- *How does grace supply what reason and will lost after the Fall?*

Chapter Sixty-five

The first secondary power, the imagination; its actions and its obedience to reason before and after original sin.

Background

In this chapter, the author tells us about the imagination, the first secondary power of the soul. Its purpose is to produce all of our images, whether they are real or imaginary. As with all powers, it is contained and comprehended in the mind. Before humanity's fall, our imagination, which never sleeps, was entirely subservient to reason and would never present the mind with unseemly images from the material or spiritual worlds. After Adam's sin, however, reason's sway over the imagination became seriously flawed, so much so that now only the assistance of grace will keep it in line. Without this influence of reason reformed by grace, the imagination would work continuously both day and night to evoke the most unseemly and fanciful images, many of which could lead to temptation and serious sin.

This disobedient and unruly nature of our imagination is seen most clearly in the recently converted who are at the beginning of their devotional lives. During their prayer time, for example, their imagination will hound them with distractions that can easily lead them away from their focus on God and tempt them with sinful thoughts and desires. It is only when reason illumined by grace regains control of the imagination through a persistent and steady regimen of prayer and meditation that these distracting images subside and eventually disappear altogether. The influence of grace on our imaginations occurs most effectively when we meditate continually on spiritual things such as our sinful, corrupted nature, the mysteries of the Incarnation, and the paschal mystery of our Lord. At the same time, it is important for us to recognize that such temptations and fanciful images are the result of original sin, the effects of which will not fully go away until the fullness of redemption takes hold in us.

TEXT

IMAGINATION is the power by which we depict the images of present and absent things. Both it and the means by which it works are contained in the mind. Before man sinned, imagination was so obedient to reason, its master, that it never pictured any perverted bodily or spiritual image. Such is not now the case. For unless it is refrained by the light of grace in reason, it will otherwise never cease in its sleeping or waking hours to portray various perverted images of bodily creatures or else some fantasy that is nothing else but a spiritual thing conceived in material terms. And this is always counterfeit and false, akin to error.

This disobedience of the imagination can be clearly seen in the prayers of those who have been recently converted from the world to a devout life. Until the imagination is controlled, for the large part, by the light of the grace of reason through the continual meditation of spiritual things—such as their own wretchedness, the passion and kindness of our Lord, and the like—they cannot overcome the great variety of thoughts, fantasies, and images imprinted in their minds by the curiosity of their imagination. All this disobedience is the result of original sin.

Entering the Cloud

- *Do you agree with the author that the imagination should be under the gentle sway of reason's rule?*

- *Do you agree that there is a major difference in the relationship between reason and the imagination before and after humanity's fall?*

- *What has been your experience of your imagination? Do you find it at times wild, unruly, and difficult to control? Have you ever felt controlled by it? Has it led you to entertain sinful thoughts and desires? What, if anything, has helped you to regain mastery over it?*

- *Have you found that keeping your mind focused on spiritual things through prayer and meditation to be of any help? Do you believe that God's grace alone will help you get it back on track?*

Chapter Sixty-six

*The other secondary power, sensuality; its activity
and obedience to the will before and after original sin.*

Background

In this chapter, the author tells us about sensuality, the other secondary power of the soul. Like the other powers, it too is contained and comprehended in the mind, as are the things it works for. Sensuality, the author tells us, deals with the bodily senses and has a twofold purpose: to look after our material needs and to serve the pleasures of our physical senses. For these reasons, it speaks out when our bodies are lacking the material things needed for subsistence and tells us to take more than what is strictly necessary in order to satisfy our desire for pleasure. It speaks up when we are deprived of things that give us pleasure and delights in their presence. It also complains when the things that displease us are in our presence and similarly takes delight in their absence.

Before humanity's fall, sensuality was a servant of the will and was completely obedient to it in all respects. It was so in tune with the will's desire to do good and to please God that it would never present it with any inordinate needs or false bodily pleasures induced by the spiritual foes of the senses. After the Fall, however, its relationship with the will became seriously disrupted. Without the influence of grace, it is now unable to refrain from lusting after the things it needs for self-preservation or that will give it instant self-gratification. Without the action of God's grace mediated through the sanctified will, it will try to take over the other powers of the soul by dragging them down to the level of pure animal pleasure, thus turning us into carnal creatures rather than the spiritual, fully human creatures we are called to become.

TEXT

SENSUALITY is a power of our soul that cares for and governs the bodily senses, through which we have sensible knowledge and feeling of the physical world creatures, whether pleasing or unpleasing. It has two roles: one that looks after our physical needs and another that provides for our physical appetites. For this same power grumbles when the body lacks the things it needs, yet when the need is met, will move it to take more than it requires to maintain and further its desires. It grumbles when its desires are not satisfied and is highly delighted when they are. It also grumbles in the presence of what revolts it and is highly pleased when it is gone. This power and the means by which it works are contained in the mind.

Before man sinned, sensuality was so obedient to the will, its master as it were, that it never led it into any perverted pleasure or pain, or any pretended spiritual pleasure or pain induced by the enemy of souls into our earthly minds. But now it is not so. Unless it is influenced by grace in the will, so that is it ready to humbly bear the consequences of original sin—which it experiences whenever it is deprived of its desired pleasures and can only have those annoying things that are good for it—and unless it reigns in both its lustful yearnings when it possesses its impure pleasures and its avaricious delight when it does not, it will wallow, like a pig in the mud, so wretchedly and savagely in the riches of the world and the filth of the flesh that the whole of its life will be animal and physical rather than human and spiritual.

Entering the Cloud

- *Do you agree with the author's description of sensuality's twofold purpose of providing for our material needs and bodily pleasures?*

- *Do you agree that sensuality's present lack of subservience to the will is a result of original sin?*

- *Do you believe that our fallen sensuality can be healed through the influence of God's grace and even elevated to a higher level to function in accordance with the will?*

- *What has your experience of sensuality been? Have you felt overpowered by certain desires for food, drink, or sexual pleasure? Have you ever felt overwhelmed, perhaps even controlled by or addicted to these and other pleasures?*

- *Have you dealt with such difficulties? Have you recognized the weakness of both your will and your sensuality to deal with these problems?*

- *Have you recognized your need for God's grace in dealing with these weaknesses? Have you ever humbly asked God for help? If not, what is keeping you from doing so?*

Chapter Sixty-seven

Unless we know the soul's powers and how they work, we may be easily deceived in our understanding of spiritual words and spiritual activity; how a soul becomes like God through grace.

Background

In this chapter, the author reminds us of the terrible effects that original sin has had on our souls. These effects have made us blind to the dangers around us and make us susceptible to mis-understanding the meaning of spiritual words and actions. This is especially true for those who have little knowledge of the soul's powers and the way they work. He reminds us that whenever we are concerned with material things, regardless of their goodness, we are acting beneath and outside ourselves. By way of contrast, whenever we are concerned with the powers of the soul and how they work in spiritual matters such as the virtues and vices, we are acting on a par with ourselves according to our nature so that we come to know ourselves better and come to perfection. Finally, whenever we are not concerned with creatures, but only with God himself, we are acting above ourselves but below God.

The author explains that the contemplative work he is proposing deals with this last level, for it concerns our desire for union with God in spirit and in will. He further explains that we are beneath God in this activity because, even though we experience oneness with him, we are still his creatures, while he is uncreated and has existed from all eternity. God, in other words, has always existed, while there was a time when we did not. He further points out that we become one with God through no merits of our own, but only through his mercy. Through our sins, we have made ourselves worse than nothing, and it is only God's forgiveness and benevolence that heals us and raises us into his presence so that we might become "gods in grace." We are one with God in grace, therefore, but far below him in nature.

For these reasons, the author wants us to be familiar with the powers of the soul and how they work in us. Otherwise, we can be easily deceived. This is also part of the reason why, earlier in the book, he asks us to act like little children and conceal our desire for union with God so that our lack of understanding would not get in the way of the work he is performing in us.

TEXT

MY spiritual friend, you can see here how to such wretchedness we have fallen through sin. Is it any wonder that we are completely and easily deceived in understanding spiritual words and activity, especially if we do not yet know the powers of our soul and their way of working?

Whenever your mind is occupied with any physical thing, however good its purpose, you are still "beneath" yourself in this activity and "outside" your soul. And whenever you feel your mind occupied with the subtleties of the soul's faculties and their spiritual activities (such as vices or virtues, in yourself or in any other spiritual creature, even with the same nature as yours) so that you might come to know yourself better and make progress in the way of perfection, you are "within" yourself and even "with" yourself. But whenever you feel your mind occupied not with physical or spiritual things, but solely with the substance of God as He is and with following the way of contemplation described in this book, then you are "above" yourself and "beneath" God.

You are "above" yourself, because you have attained by grace what you could not attain by nature. That is to say, you have become united to God in spirit and love and harmony of will. You are "beneath" your God because in a manner of speaking you and God at this time can be said to be not two but one in spirit—so that you or anyone else who reaches the perfection of contemplation may, because of this unity may be called a "god," as Scripture itself testifies [21]—nevertheless you are still "beneath" Him. For He is God by nature without beginning, yet you were once nothing at all. And when afterward you were created by His power and love, you by your deliberate act of willful sinning made yourself less than nothing. And it is only by His undeserved mercy that you are made a god by grace, inseparably united to Him in spirit, both here and in the bliss of heaven, world without end! Although you may be entirely one with Him in grace, you are still infinitely far below Him in nature.

My spiritual friend, you can now see, at least in part, whoever does not know the powers of their own soul and the way they work can very easily be deceived in understanding the meaning of words that are written with spiritual intent. And you may also see something of the reason why I begged you like a child to do all you could to conceal your longing for God rather than speak of it openly. I do for fear you would understand physically what is intended spiritually.

Entering the Cloud

- *Do you agree that original sin has wreaked havoc on the human soul? Do you think you understand the full effects of this sin of human origins on humanity?*

- *How has this sin manifested itself in your life? How has it affected the powers of your soul: reason, will, imagination, and sensuality? How has it affected your relationship with God, with others, and with yourself?*

- *Do you understand what the author means when he says we are acting beneath and outside ourselves, on par with and within ourselves, above ourselves but beneath God? On which of these levels do you normally live? On which of these levels would you like to live?*

- *Do you believe that intimate union with God comes about only through God's forgiveness and the influence of his grace? Have you ever asked for his mercy and grace?*

- *Do you understand why the author asked his readers earlier to hide their desires from God like little children?*

- *How can our lack of self-knowledge get in the way of our spiritual journey?*

Chapter Sixty-eight

Nowhere physically is everywhere spiritually;
our outer nature looks upon the work of this book as nothing.

Background

In this chapter, the author tells us that our bodily senses will not lead us along the contemplative way he is describing and that it would be better for us to focus on being "nowhere" than in some physical place and time. He even cautions us against the otherwise sound advice of worshiping God interiorly by gathering all our faculties and powers within ourselves. He does so for fear of our mistaking a spiritual place for a physical, earthly one. He reminds us that in seeking to penetrate the cloud of unknowing we must try not to be physically outside, above, behind, beside, or even within ourselves. Instead, we must strive to be nowhere, for to be nowhere bodily is to be everywhere spiritually. We are to cast everything related to the bodily senses into the cloud of forgetting so that our search for God will not be misled by false bodily interpretations of words packed full of spiritual meaning. He tells us not to worry if our bodily senses find nothing nourishing in this spiritual nowhere and asks us to simply carry on our search for God's love in the midst of this nothingness. He encourages us to press on with our search and asks us to be led by nothing but our desire for God.

It is much better for us to wrestle with this blind nothingness than to be surrounded by the things of this world like a king and his possessions. We are to leave everything aside in order to enter this nowhere, which will seem dark and obscure to those just beginning their contemplative search for this elusive God. Because of our inexperience, we will at first feel blinded by the deep spiritual light emanating from this place of nowhere. In time, however, we will experience a profound change. The inner man will begin to experience what the outward man could not: The darkness will turn to light, the nothing will become everything, and the nowhere will become All. Our inner self comes alive in this search. Blessed with a sound understanding of both the physical and spiritual worlds, it is able to see both how they relate and how they are separate from one another.

TEXT

IN the same way, when another man tells you to gather all your powers and thoughts within yourself and worship God there— although what he says is absolutely true—I tell you not to do so, for fear of being deceived through a physical interpretation of his words. But I will tell you this. Make sure that you in no way withdraw into yourself. In short, I do not want you to be "outside," "above," "behind," or "beside" yourself.

"Where then," you say, "shall I be? Nowhere, according to you!" You would indeed be right, for nowhere is where I want you to be. When you are "nowhere" physically, you are "everywhere" spiritually. Make sure that your spiritual work is nowhere physically, and you will see that wherever that thing is that occupies your mind, there you are in spirit, just as your body is where you are physically. Although your natural mind can find there "nothing" to feed on, for it thinks you are doing nothing, continue doing this nothing and do it for the love of God. So do not relent, but work earnestly on that nothing, with a waking desire and will to have God, whom no one knows. For I tell you truly that I would much rather be nowhere physically, wrestling with that dark nothing, than a great lord who could go anywhere he wanted and enjoy everything as if it were his own.

Let go of this "everywhere" and "everything" and embrace this "nowhere" and "nothing." So what if you cannot understand anything of this "nothing." Surely you will love it so much more. It is so worthwhile in itself that reason cannot give it its due. This "nothing" can be better felt than seen, for it is completely dark and obscure when looked upon. Still, to speak more clearly, a soul is more blinded by feeling the abundance of spiritual light than by the darkness or absence of spiritual light. Who is it then who calls it "nothing?" Surely it is our outer self, not our inner self. Our inner self calls it "All," for through it he is learning the nature of all physical and spiritual things without needing to consider any one thing by itself.

Entering the Cloud

- *Why does the author distrust the bodily senses as a means to the spiritual? Is it because of their capacity to lead us astray? Is it because of the effects of original sin?*

- *Can the bodily senses lead us beyond themselves? Have you ever experienced the spiritual through the physical? Have you ever experienced this place of nowhere of which the author speaks? Have you ever felt as though you were out of your bodily senses, being neither outside, above, behind, beside, or even within yourself?*

- *Have you had a sense of your own nothingness, feeling blinded by all that surrounds you? Have you ever experienced this darkness turned to light?*

- *Are you more in touch with your outward self or inward self? With which do you feel more comfortable?*

Chapter Sixty-nine

How a person's affections are marvelously changed in the spiritual experience of this nothing, which occurs nowhere.

Background

In this chapter, the author tells us how our affections are changed when we enter this place of nowhere. When we first experience the nothingness of the cloud of unknowing, we usually have a deep sense of our sinfulness. The particular sins of our past rise up to haunt us and will leave us only after we shed many bitter tears. We feel as though we are looking upon hell itself, and we wonder if we will ever escape its torments. The spiritual consolation we so desperately seek seems a long way off, and many of us will turn from the path of unknowing and seek comfort in outward, material things. If we have patience, however, we will find that the influence of grace removes many of these particular sins, and we will experience some degree of the consolation and hope for perfection for which we long. In time, what once seemed like hell will now appear like purgatory. Our particular sins will seem more like a lump of sin, which comes from our sinful nature and the effects of original sin. At other times, we will experience so many joys and consolations that we feel like we are in heaven. At still other times, it seems as though God himself has reached out his hand and showered us with peace and rest. Even as our affections are transformed in this experience of nothing, the author reminds us that there will always be a cloud of unknowing between us and God.

TEXT

A MAN'S affections are greatly varied in the spiritual experience of this nothing wrought from nowhere. When a soul first looks upon it, he finds that all the sins he committed since birth, whether physical or spiritual, secret or somber, are imprinted on it. They meet his gaze wherever he turns, until the time comes when, with much difficult travail and with many aching sighs and bitter tears, he has in large part washed them away. During this struggle, he sometimes thinks he is beholding hell itself, for he thinks that, because of that suffering, he has lost all hope of ever reaching the perfection of spiritual rest. Many come this far in their spiritual journey, but because their suffering is great and they have no relief, they go back to the consideration of worldly things. They seek out external fleshly comforts for lack of the spiritual ones they have not yet deserved, as they would have if they had endured.

For he who endures sometimes feels comfort and has some hope of perfection, for he begins to feel and to see that many of his past sins are to a great extent being rubbed away by grace. Though he still has to suffer, he thinks that it will one day come to an end, for it is always becoming less and less. So he sees it as a purgatory. Sometimes he can find no particular sin written there, though he still thinks of sin as a "lump," which he does not examine but knows to be nothing but himself. Then it may be called the basis and the painful outcome of original sin. Sometimes he believes it to be paradise or heaven because of the varied and wonderful delights, comforts, joys, and blessed virtues he finds there. Sometimes he believes it is God, for such is the peace and rest he finds there.

Yes, whatever he thinks, he will always find a cloud of unknowing between him and God.

Entering the Cloud

- *Do you agree with the author's description of the change in affection that comes about through this spiritual exercise? Does it correspond to your own experience?*

- *Why are our affections changed as a result of our entering the cloud of unknowing? How are they transformed? Is it because the experience of nothingness puts us in touch with our own nothingness? Is it because the cloud of unknowing helps us to see ourselves as we truly are?*

- *Is the consciousness of our sinfulness changed because we have been given a deeper sense of God's mercy and forgiveness?*

Chapter Seventy

*Silencing our bodily senses enables us to arrive more easily
at a knowledge of spiritual things; in like manner, silencing
our spiritual faculties enables us, as much as grace allows us
on earth, to come to an experiential knowledge of God.*

Background

In this chapter, the author tells us that abstinence from the bodily
senses will help us in the experience of spiritual things, while the
quieting of our spiritual powers will lead us to an experiential,
face-to-face encounter with God. He points out that the purpose
of our bodily senses is to increase our knowledge of the material
world, not the spiritual. Our senses of sight, hearing, smell, taste,
and touch are not equipped to actively tell us anything about the
spiritual world. We can gain insight into this dimension of reality
through these senses only by their lack of activity. For example, we
may wish to confirm something we have read or heard about the
spiritual world and the inability of our senses to tell us anything
about it points to something beyond the material. In a similar
way, our spiritual faculties can tell us a great deal about created
spiritual things but little if anything about God, who is an uncreated spiritual being. It is only by their failure, through their lack
of activity, that our spiritual senses point beyond themselves and
show us something by the way of unknowing. To verify his claim,
he refers us to Dionysius the Areopagite, although he does not cite
any specific works since he believes doing so would be a needless
display of learning. He simply asks his readers to listen to his words
and to seek God in the cloud of unknowing through the quieting
of their bodily and spiritual senses.

WORK hard and fast in this nothing and this nowhere, and leave your outward physical senses and their activities. For I truly tell you that you cannot understand this work of contemplation through them.

With your eyes you can only understand something by its appearance: whether it is long or wide, small or large, round or square, far or near or colored. With your ears you understand by noise or sound; with your nose by the stench or scent; with your taste whether something is sour or sweet, salt or fresh, bitter or pleasant; with your touch whether it is hot or cold, hard or soft, blunt or sharp. But God and spiritual things have none of these qualities or quantities. So leave your outward senses and do not work with them either objectively or subjectively. For if those who wish to become spiritual and inward-looking contemplatives believe they ought to hear, smell, see, taste, or feel spiritual things in external visions or in the depth of their being, they are greatly deceived and are working against the course of nature.

For by nature it is ordained that through the senses men should have knowledge of all outward physical things, but in no way does a knowledge of spiritual things come through them. I mean through the activity of the senses. By acknowledging their limitations, however, we may attain such knowledge. For example, when we hear or read of certain things and see that our natural understanding cannot adequately describe what they are, then we may be quite sure that those things are spiritual and not physical.

The same thing happens spiritually when we try to come to a knowledge of God using our spiritual senses. For even if a man is deeply versed in the understanding and knowledge of all created spiritual things, he can never by such understanding come to know an uncreated spiritual thing—which is nothing else than God! But by recognizing the reason for the limitation, he may. Because the thing that limits his understanding is God, Himself alone. That is why St. Dionysius said, "The most spiritual knowledge of God is that which is known by unknowing." Indeed, whoever reads Dionysius' works will find that he clearly endorses all I have said or shall say from the beginning of this treatise to the end. Other than this, I do not bother to quote him now or any other authority as well. Men once thought it was humble to say nothing original unless they could support it with Scripture and the words of learned men. Today the practice provides the occasion for displaying one's curiosity and cunning. It is not necessary for you, and so I do not do it. For whoever has ears, let him hear, and whoever is moved to believe, let him believe. There is no other way.

Entering the Cloud

- *Do you agree that the bodily senses tell us very little, if anything, about the spiritual realm?*

- *Do you agree that we can gain more insight into the spiritual when the body's senses are calm?*

- *Do you agree that the activity of the spiritual powers reveals much about created spiritual things but little if anything about God?*

- *Do you agree that we can experience God when we quiet the spiritual senses through the way of unknowing?*

- *Have you ever experienced God in this way? Is this something that can be planned or must it simply be accepted when it comes?*

Chapter Seventy-one

Some may experience the perfection of contemplation during ecstasy; others, at will and in their normal state of consciousness.

Background

In this chapter, the author tells us that some people will experience God through this spiritual exercise only when in the state of ecstasy, while others will experience him whenever they wish during their usual state of awareness. He tries to explain this discrepancy by pointing to the order and disposition of God. Experiencing God in the cloud of unknowing is a mystical experience that depends on God's initiative, not our own. There is nothing we can do to bring about such an experience in our lives. Even the regular exercise of casting all thought into the cloud of forgetting and then knocking on the cloud of unknowing will not make it happen. All it will do is prepare us to receive God's action in our lives and help us to recognize it when it comes.

As far as the experience itself is concerned, this depends entirely on the divine initiative and cannot be predicted by human means. The author points to the Ark of the Covenant as the symbol par excellence for this mystical experience and reminds us that Moses had to prepare himself with long labor before he could see the Ark, while his brother, Aaron, could enter it virtually at will by virtue of his office (see Exodus 24:15 and appropriate verses that follow). In a similar way, God ordains that some will experience him mystically only on rare occasions when standing outside of themselves in the state of ecstasy, while he allows others to experience him on a more regular basis, while in their normal state of consciousness. It bears noting, moreover, that experiencing God face-to-face in a mystical experience is not a prerequisite for holiness. Many progress along the way of holiness without ever having had such an experience in this life and will do so only when they reach the state of perfection in the world to come.

TEXT

SOME consider this matter of contemplation so difficult and fearsome that they say it cannot be accomplished without a great deal of very hard work beforehand and that it occurs infrequently, and then only in the state of ecstasy. To these men I respond as best I can and say that it all happens according to God's will and good pleasure according to their capacity to receive this grace of contemplation and the work of the Spirit.

Without a doubt, some cannot attain this state without long and hard spiritual work beforehand, and even then it happens only rarely and in response to a special call from our Lord called the state of ecstasy.

There are others, however, who by grace are so sensitive in spirit and so at home with God in this grace of contemplation that they can have it when they like and under normal conditions, whether they are sitting, walking, standing, or kneeling. At such times, they have complete command of their physical and spiritual faculties and can use them as they wish, although not without some difficulty (but without great difficulty). We have an example of the first kind in Moses, and of the second in Aaron, the priest of the temple. As the story shows, the grace of contemplation is prefigured in the Old Law by the Ark of the Covenant and contemplatives by those who cared for it. This grace and work of contemplation may be likened to the Ark because it contained all the jewels and relics of the Temple, as our little love focused on this cloud of unknowing contains all the virtues of a man's, the spiritual temple of God.

Before Moses could see the Ark and learn how it should be constructed, he had to climb to the top of the mountain through long, strenuous effort, remain six days in a cloud and wait until our Lord descended from heaven on the seventh day to show him how to build it. [22] Moses' hard work and his delayed vision represent those who cannot reach the perfection of contemplation without much effort and toil beforehand and, even then, they experience it but seldom and only when God so desires.

Although Moses could only "see" on occasion and not without great effort, Aaron, by virtue of his office, had it in his power to see God in the Temple behind the veil whenever he entered. Aaron represents all those I have just mentioned who, because of their spiritual wisdom and by the help of grace, experience perfect contemplation whenever they wish.

Entering the Cloud

- *Have you ever had a mystical experience of God? If so, what was it like? How would you describe it? Did it occur only rarely, in an "out of the body" experience, in what the author calls a state of ecstasy? Or has it occurred more frequently in your life, as part of your normal, day-to-day consciousness?*

- *Is there only one type of mystical experience or many?*

- *Can you identify with the author's use of the Ark of the Covenant for describing the nature of mystical experience?*

- *Do you agree that, like Moses and Aaron, different people may be blessed by God with different frequencies of this experience?*

- *Do you see the distinction between holiness and mystical experience and recognize that some people will see God face-to-face only in the afterlife?*

- *Do you consider yourself a mystic? If not, do you desire holiness? How would you describe the difference?*

Chapter Seventy-two

Those who regularly practice this work of contemplation should not presume that other contemplatives experience exactly what they do.

Background

In this chapter, the author asks us not to assume other contemplatives will have the same experience when penetrating the cloud of unknowing. He says it is wrong to judge others from our own experience. If we come to this mystical, face-to-face encounter with God only after much toil and labor, we should not be alarmed if others come to it more easily and in their normal state of awareness. Similarly, if we experience God in this way on a regular basis, we should not judge others who receive it less frequently or perhaps not at all. He asks us not to make our own contemplative experience the basis for judging the authenticity of others. It is wrong to think this way, since God alone dispenses this intimate experience of himself according to his own good pleasure. If God so desired, those who were used to experiencing him regularly in this way might receive it less frequently—and vice versa. He points to Moses as an example of someone who, at first, entered this mystical state only rarely and with great toil, but who later was permitted by God to receive it with great ease and regularity (see Exodus 33:7–11).

TEXT

BY this you can see that the man who attains and experiences perfect contemplation after much effort but only on occasion may be easily deceived if he speaks, thinks, or judges by his own experience, thinking that others can only attain it rarely and not without great effort. In the same way, the man who can attain it whenever he wishes may also be deceived if he judges by his own criteria and thinks others can have it whenever they like. Surely he should not think this way. If God so pleases, it may well be that those who achieve it but seldom and not without great effort shall afterward have it when they will and as often as they like. Take Moses, for example. On the mountaintop, he at first saw the Ark only rarely and not without great effort, but later he saw it in the valley as often as he desired.

Entering the Cloud

- *Do you agree that no one but God can bestow the experience of his innermost, contemplative life on others? If this is so, then why should we even bother with the spiritual exercises suggested in this book?*

- *Could it be that God uses such exercises to prepare us for this intense mystical experience? Are there other ways in which he might prepare us?*

- *Why does God bestow this mystical experience on some with great frequency, on others only rarely, and on still others not at all?*

- *Where would you place yourself along this spectrum?*

- *How does cooperation with God's grace lead us along the path of holiness? How does it lead us along the path of intimate divine friendship?*

Chapter Seventy-three

The Ark of the Covenant prefigures the grace available for us in contemplation in three ways and is based on how Moses, Bezalel, and Aaron deal with it.

Background

In this chapter, the author extends his analogy of the Ark of the Covenant as a biblical foreshadowing of the grace of contemplation and points specifically to three figures—Moses, Bezalel, and Aaron—as concrete examples of the different ways we experience God in the cloud of unknowing. In doing so, he develops his insights from previous chapters about the kinds of contemplatives who use this exercise from two to three. On the top of Mount Sinai, Moses received instructions about how the Ark should be made (see Exodus 25:10–22). Below in the valley, Bezalel fashioned the Ark according to instructions received by Moses (see Exodus 36:1–38). Within the Temple, Aaron had the Ark in his keeping and could touch it as often as he liked. Using these figures as the basis for his analogy, the author tells us that we grow in the grace of contemplation in similar ways.

Like Moses, some receive this experience only through the influence of God's grace and, regardless of their hard work and ascetical preparation, come to it only rarely and in God's own time. Like Bezalel, others receive this experience not only through the influence of God's grace but also through their own spiritual skill. They build on the instructions given to others and are very adept at explaining and implementing the spiritual plan they have received. Finally, like Aaron, others benefit from both the spiritual foundations laid by others and God's good pleasure. Because they follow this office closely and keep it close to their hearts, God allows them to enter the cloud of unknowing with great regularity and to experience him at will. In each of these examples, God's grace figures as the determining factor, although cooperation with this grace, use of one's spiritual skill, and adherence to one's spiritual office also enter into the mix. The author, we might add, identifies himself with Bezalel, that is, as someone capable of fashioning a teaching on the cloud of unknowing for others to use and implement far better than he and to much greater avail.

TEXT

THERE were three men who most dealt with the Ark of the Old Testament: Moses, Bezalel, and Aaron. Moses learned on the mountain of our Lord how it should be made. Bezalel labored and constructed it in the valley according to the prescriptions revealed on the mountain. And Aaron cared for it in the Temple to handle it and see it as often as he liked.

We can see in these three a representation of the three ways in which the grace of contemplation can help us. Sometimes our profit comes only through grace, and then we are like Moses, who for all his climbing and effort on the mountain was able to see it only rarely and only when it pleased our Lord to reveal it, and not as a reward for all his toil. Sometimes our profit comes as the result of our own spiritual skill, with the help of God's grace, and then we are like Bezalel, who could not see the Ark before he had made it by his own efforts but was assisted by the plan revealed to Moses on the mountain. And sometimes our profit in this grace comes through other men's teaching, and then we are like Aaron, who cared for the Ark and who was accustomed to see and handle what Bezalel had constructed beforehand whenever he wished.

My spiritual friend, though I speak childishly and foolishly in this work and, wretch that I am, am unworthy to teach anyone, I bear the office of Bezalel, making and placing in your care something akin to a spiritual Ark. But you will have to work far better and more worthily than I if you wish to be like Aaron, that is to say, by continually working at it for your sake—and mine! Go on then, I beg you, for the love of God Almighty. And since we are both called by God to the work of contemplation, I beg you, for the love of God, to fulfill on your part what is lacking in mine.

Entering the Cloud

- *Do you agree with the author's extended use of Moses, Bezalel, and Aaron as a way of depicting the various ways which we can make use of the grace of contemplation?*

- *What are the strengths and weaknesses of such an allegorical interpretation? With which figure do you identify the most? Do you perhaps identify a little with all three?*

- *Do you agree with the author's self-identification with the role of Bezalel? From what you have read, do you see a little of Moses or possibly even Aaron in him?*

- *Can you think of any other biblical passages or figures that can be used as a basis for describing the contemplative experience to today's readers?*

Chapter Seventy-four

*A soul properly disposed to contemplation cannot read or
speak of the contents of this book, or hear it read or spoken
about, without feeling suited to this work and its effects;
a summary of the same direction given in the prologue.*

Background

In this chapter, the author reiterates the instructions given in the
prologue about the audience for whom the book is intended. He
reaffirms the contemplative nature of his work and asks that it be
kept out of the hands of those with little or no interest in living
the Gospel on this deep level of awareness. He specifically refers
to those members of the clergy and laity who may excel in matters
pertaining to the active life but have little or no interest in fostering their own interior lives. He does not present his insights into
the contemplative life as the only way to an intimate experience
of God and tells us to put them aside in good conscience if we do
not feel drawn to them and have received sound spiritual counsel
to do so. He asserts, moreover, that his only intention in writing
the book was to help us progress in the spiritual life according to
the insights God has granted him.

The author acknowledges the difficulty of these insights and,
for this reason, suggests that the book be read several times over
(the more often the better)—and in its entirety. In keeping with
the author's monastic background, it seems clear that he wants his
readers to ponder the text slowly through the contemplative approach of lectio divina rather than the more intellectual, dialectical
approach championed by the scholastics. To be sure, he intends
his insights to penetrate to the heart and not to remain on the
level of conceptual thought, a dimension of human knowledge of
which he is deeply suspicious. One of his great fears is that a partial
reading of the book will lead his readers into misunderstandings

and possibly even great error about the spiritual life. He says this because the cumulative (as opposed to linear) effect of the work and his forward-looking intuition that a knowledge of the whole is necessary for a proper understanding the individual parts.

Aware that his work will pass through many hands, he warns his intended readers of this danger and asks them to have immediate recourse to him should any part of his teaching be in need of clarification. Be that as it may, he is convinced that his insights into the cloud will resonate in the hearts of those called to this work. These contemplatives, he believes, will not be able to hear or read about this work, whether aloud or in private, without feeling a deep affinity for it and its effects.

TEXT

IF you think that this work of contemplation does not fit your physical or spiritual disposition, then you may leave it and, with good spiritual counsel, safely follow another without blame. In that case, I ask you to excuse me, for my sincere intention was to help you as far as my simple knowledge would allow. Therefore, read this book over two or three times (the more often, the better), for you will come to understand it better. Some sentence, perhaps, that was too hard for you at the first or second reading will afterward be found easy.

Yes, I find it is impossible to see how any soul disposed to contemplation could read or speak about this work, or hear it read or spoken of, without feeling a very genuine affection and concern for its outcome. So, if you find it helpful, give thanks to God and, for love of Him, pray for me.

So go on. And I beg you, for the love of God, let no one see this book unless he is, in your judgment, able to profit from it in the way I described earlier. If you do let anyone see it, I beg you to bid them to give themselves time to look it all over carefully. For there may be some matter at the beginning or in the middle which is left hanging and not fully explained where it stands. If it is not dealt with there, it will be soon afterward, or at the end. If a man saw only one part of the matter and not the other, he might easily be led into error; therefore, I beg you to do as I say. And if you think you need more instruction on any matter within, let me know what it is and what your thoughts are on it, and I will do my best to explain.

Still, I do not want any earthy janglers, flatterers and blamers, ronkers and ronners, and all manner of pinchers to see to this book, for it was never my intention to write any of this for them. I would rather they did not hear it, and the same goes for those learned (and unlearned) people who are merely curious. Yes, even if they are good men from an active standpoint, none of this will mean anything to them.

Entering the Cloud

- *Do you agree that this book is not intended for everyone?*
- *Do you agree that it could do great damage to a person's spiritual life if taken out of context and not read in its entirety?*
- *Do you agree that it needs to be read contemplatively, in the style of lectio divina, rather than analytically and for its content?*
- *Who would benefit most from reading this book? To whom would you recommend it?*
- *Can the author's "way of unknowing" stand alone? Does it appear strange that he uses words, images, and ideas— the building blocks of thought—to convey a message that encourages us to abandon thought and embark upon an entirely different way of knowing?*

Chapter Seventyfive

Some certain signs by which we may know whether we are called by God to the contemplative life.

Background

In this final chapter, the author gives us some advice on how to determine whether we are called to practice this way of unknowing. He begins by warning us that we should not assume we are called to this way of contemplation simply because we have a good feeling and are attracted to it when reading about it. Such feelings can stem from intellectual curiosity rather than grace. He then points out a number of positive signs to look for that will help us determine whether such feelings are rooted in grace and represent a call from God.

In the first place, we must do everything possible to cleanse our consciences according to the instructions of the Church (that is, sacramental reconciliation) and the counsel of their spiritual directors. Secondly, we must ask ourselves if the impulse to pray in this way occupies our thoughts more than any other spiritual or devotional exercises. Thirdly, we must ask ourselves if we truly believe that nothing else we do is of any value when compared with this "secret love" of the way of unknowing. If we have a deep sense that our most important task in life is to penetrate this cloud, then God may well be calling us to this contemplative activity. To put it another way, the author is telling us that if we have not taken the time to clear our consciences, reconcile ourselves with God and his Church, seek the counsel of our spiritual directors, examine the depth and intensity of our desires regarding this spiritual exercise, and come to the conclusion that it is our primary task in life, then we are most likely not called by God to embark on this journey. At the same time, the author does not mean to say that we must always be conscious of this deep stirring in our hearts. He reminds us that this desire may sometimes be taken from our hearts so that we do not become overly familiar with it. Otherwise, out of pride, we may come to feel that it is something under our own control rather than God's. In such cases, we may become angry with God for taking this desire from our hearts and see him as an enemy, when he is actually our best friend trying to help us avoid making a serious mistake.

In addition to pride, the author tells us that the loss of this desire can also be due to carelessness. We may become so familiar with this longing to penetrate the cloud that we take it for granted. God, in turn, may deliberately delay the desire in order to expand and deepen it in our hearts so that we may experience it anew after a long absence. The author then gives us a fourth sign to help us determine if God is calling us to this exercise. He says that, after a long absence, it may suddenly resurface in our hearts without any outside help. We may find that we receive this experience with great longing and that our desire for this work of contemplation is greater than ever before. We may also see that our joy in finding it once more is far greater than our sorrow in losing it. If these be our experiences in finding this desire once again, then it is clear that God is calling us to this exercise.

The author is quick to point out that this calling depends not on what we are or what we have become, but on what we desire. He cites Gregory the Great to remind us that holy desires grow when taken from us and that they could never be considered holy if they decreased after a long absence. He also cites St. Augustine to remind us that the whole of Christian life consists of nothing but fostering holy desires. He concludes this chapter (and the book) by bidding us farewell, by invoking God's blessing upon us, and by asking that God's peace, counsel, comfort, and abundant grace be with us, and all who love God—forever.

TEXT

ALL who read this book, or hear it read or spoken of, and as a result think it a good and pleasant thing, are not necessarily called by God to take up this work, simply because of the pleasant experience they get from reading it. Such a conclusion may come more from a natural curiosity than from a call of grace.

But, if they want to test the origin of this desire, they can try this out if they wish. First let them see if they have done all that is necessary beforehand, readying themselves by cleansing their conscience according to the law of Holy Church and the advice of their director. It is good that they do this. If they wish to know more, let them see whether this desire claims their attention constantly, habitually, more than other spiritual exercises. And if they think nothing they do, physically or spiritually, is done in accordance with their conscience, unless this secret little love fixed on the cloud of unknowing is the main thrust of all their spiritual work, and if they truly feel this, then it is a sign that they are called by God to this work. Otherwise, it is not.

I am not saying that this desire lasts forever and that it dwells continually in the minds of those called to this work. It is not so. For the desire itself is, for various reasons, often withdrawn from a beginning contemplative. Sometimes it happens so he will not presume too much and think that it lies within his power to have it as often as he pleases. Such presumption is pride. Whenever the feeling of grace is withdrawn, pride is always the cause; not necessarily actual pride but potential pride that would have arisen if the feeling had not been withdrawn. Because of this, there are some young fools who think God is their enemy, when in fact he is their best friend.

Sometimes it is withdrawn because of their carelessness. When this happens, they experience a deep pain that bites into them bitterly like an open sore. Sometimes our Lord delays the feeling of grace on purpose because He wants such delays to make it grow and be more highly valued, which is what happens when something long lost is found. And here is one of the surest and most important signs a soul can have to determine whether or not he is called to contemplation. After a delay of this sort and a long absence, the ability to contemplate comes back suddenly and unsought for, and he has a burning desire and a deeper passion for contemplation than ever before. So much so, that I often think his joy at its recovery far outweighs his sorrow at its loss! If this is so, it is surely a true and unmistakable sign that he has been called by God to become a contemplative, whatever he might have once been, or may still be.

For it is not what you are or have been that God looks at with His merciful eyes, but what you would be. St. Gregory tells us, "all holy desires grow by delays; and if they fade because of these delays, then they were never holy desires." If a man feels ever less joy in new findings and in the sudden increases in his former desires for good, then those desires were never holy. Saint Augustine speaks of this holy desire when he says, "The life of a good Christian consists of nothing else but holy desire."

Farewell, my spiritual friend! May God's blessing and mine be upon you. I ask Almighty God that true peace, holy counsel, spiritual comfort, and an abundance of grace be always with you and with all His lovers on the earth. Amen.

Here ends *The Cloud of Unknowing.*

Entering the Cloud

- *Do you agree that the contemplative exercise of penetrating the cloud of unknowing depends on a call from God?*

- *Do you believe this call is extended to many or to only an elite few? How does it differ from the normal Christian call to discipleship?*

- *Do you believe you have received this call?*

- *Do you agree that interest in the call can stem from natural intellectual curiosity rather than God's grace?*

- *Do you agree with the four signs given by the author for helping us discern whether we have this call? Do you disagree with any of them? Would you add any others to the list?*

- *Do you agree that God looks upon us with merciful eyes and that it is not what we are or have become but our desires that are important in the spiritual life?*

- *Do you agree that our desire for holiness is ultimately a gift from God?*

- *Do you agree that we may sometimes lose this longing out of pride or carelessness? Can you think of any other factors that could contribute to our loss of this longing?*

- *Do you believe that holy desires increase over time, even when they are absent for a while?*

- *Do you believe that the Christian life is ultimately about fostering holy desires? Do you foster such desires? Is your deepest desire in life to become holy? Do you long to be a saint?*

- *Is this God's will for you?*

Endnotes

1. Thomas Keating, *Open Heart, Open Mind: The Contemplative Dimension of the Gospel* (Amity, NY: Amity House, 1986), 109, 114.

2. The author of *The Cloud of Unknowing* was under the general impression of the time (not disproven until the sixteenth century) that the Dionysian corpus of mystical writings carried great spiritual authority because they were the work of a convert and disciple of St. Paul's, one of Christianity's greatest apostles. In the Middle Ages, the Dionysius of Acts 17 and the early sixth-century "Pseudo-Dionysius" were thought to be one and the same person and were often identified with St. Dionysius (Denis), the third-century bishop and martyr of Paris. This lack of historical consciousness was not uncommon in medieval times and would not be rectified until the Renaissance and the birth of the modern era.

3. *The Cloud of Unknowing,* chapter 70 (see No. 6 below).

4. Augustine of Hippo, *In Epistolam Joannis ad Parthos,* 6.6.

5. *The Cloud of Unknowing,* preface (see No. 6 below).

6. Evelyn Underhill, ed., *The Cloud of Unknowing,* with an introduction by Evelyn Underhill, 2d ed. (London: John M. Watkins, 1922). Edited from the British Museum MS. Harl. 674.

7. William A. Meninger, *The Loving Search for God: Contemplative Prayer and* The Cloud of Unknowing (New York: Continuum, 1994), xvii.

8. See James Walsh, "Introduction," in *The Cloud of Unknowing,* ed. James Walsh, The Classics of Western Spirituality (New York/Ramsey/Toronto: Paulist Press, 1981), 100 n.2. For arguments against the author being a Carthusian, see Idem, "Introduction," 2-9.

9. See James Walsh, "Introduction," 116n. 14.

10. *Ibid.*

11. See Luke 10:42.

12. See Matthew 5:48.

13. Although they were often conflated in medieval times, Mary Magdalene, Mary of Bethany, and the woman caught in adultery are today considered distinct figures.

14. See Luke 10:40–42.

15. See Luke 10:41–42.

16. See John 20:11–13.

17. See Luke 7:44.

18. See Exodus 19:13 and Hebrews 12:20.

19. See John 3:13.

20. See Philippians 3:20.

21. See John 10:34.

22. See Exodus 25.

Suggested Reading

Editions of The Cloud of Unknowing

Hodgson, Phyllis, ed. *The Cloud of Unknowing.* London: Early English Text Society, 1944; OUP, 1958.

Johnston, William, ed. *The Cloud of Unknowing* and *The Book of Privy Counseling.* Introduction by William Johnston. Garden City, NY: Doubleday, 1973.

Progoff, Ira, trans. *The Cloud of Unknowing.* Introduction by Ira Progoff. New York: Delta Publishing, Co., 1957; 1st Delta printing, 1973.

McCann, Augustine, ed. T*he Cloud of Unknowing and Other Treatises.* With a commentary on *The Cloud* by Augustine Baker. 6th ed. Westminster, MD: The Newman Press, 1952.

Underhill, Evelyn, ed. *The Cloud of Unknowing.* Introduction by Evelyn Underhill. 2d ed. London: John M. Watkins, 1922.

Walsh, James, ed. *The Cloud of Unknowing.* Preface by Simon Tugwell. Introduction by James Walsh. The Classics of Western Spirituality. New York: Paulist Press, 1981.

Wolters, Clifton., trans. *The Cloud of Unknowing and Other Works.* Introduction by Clifton Wolters. Harmondsworth and New York: Penguin Books, 1961, 1978.

Other Works

Armstrong, Karen. *Vision of God: Four Medieval Mystics and Their Writings*. New York: Bantam Books, 1994.

Clark, John P. H. "The Cloud of Unknowing." Chapter in *An Introduction to the Medieval Mystics of Europe*. Edited by Paul E. Szarmach. Albany, NY: State University of New York Press, 1984.

Hodgson, Phyllis. *Three 14th-Century English Mystics*. London: Longmans, 1967.

Johnston, William. *The Mysticism of* The Cloud of Unknowing: *A Modern Interpretation*. New York: Harper & Row, 1967.

Keating, Thomas. *Foundations for Centering Prayer and the Christian Contemplative Life: Open Mind, Open Heart; The Mystery of Christ*. New York: Continuum, 2002.

_____. *Open Mind, Open Heart: The Contemplative Dimension of the Gospel*. Amity, NY: Amity House, 1986.

Meninger, William A. *The Loving Search for God: Contemplative Prayer and* The Cloud of Unknowing. New York: Continuum, 1994.

Pennington, M. Basil. *Centered Living: The Way of Centering Prayer*. Liguori, MO: Liguori Publications, 2002.

_____. *Centering Prayer: Renewing an Ancient Christian Prayer Form*. Garden City, NY: Doubleday, 1982.

Underhill, Evelyn. *Mystics of the Church*. Cambridge: James Clarke & Co. LTD, 1925; reprinted 1975.

Wolters, Clifton. "The English Mystics." Chapter in *The Study of Spirituality*, eds. Chesslyn Jones, Geoffrey Wainwright, Edward Yarnold. London: SPCK, 1992.

CPSIA information can be obtained at www.ICGtesting.com
Printed in the USA
LVOW10s2312040514

384315LV00001B/1/P